GUIDE FOR CELEBRATING
THE PASTORAL
CARE OF THE SICK

J. PHILIP HORRIGAN

LTP
LITURGY
TRAINING
PUBLICATIONS

Nihil Obstat
Rev. Mr. Daniel G. Welter, JD
Chancellor
Archdiocese of Chicago
February 27, 2019

Imprimatur
Most Rev. Ronald A. Hicks
Vicar General
Archdiocese of Chicago
February 27, 2019

The *Nihil Obstat* and *Imprimatur* are declarations that the material is free from doctrinal or moral error, and thus is granted permission to publish in accordance with c. 827. No legal responsibility is assumed by the grant of this permission. No implication is contained herein that those who have granted the Nihil Obstat and Imprimatur agree with the content, opinions, or statements expressed.

This book is part of the Preparing Parish Worship series.

This book was edited by Danielle A. Noe. Christian Rocha was the production editor, Anna Manhart was the series and cover designer, and Juan Alberto Castillo was the production artist.

Cover photography by Anna Manhart and Andrew Kennedy Lewis © Liturgy Training Publications. Interior photo on page 115 © Karen Callaway; photo on page 25 © Catholic News Agency; photos on pages 78 and 100 by Ramazan Durmus © Liturgy Training Publications; photos on pages 38, 40, 43, 46, 51, 53, 58, 76, 85, 93, 101, 121, 125, 127, and 138 by Mark Hollopeter © Liturgy Training Publications; photo on page 98 by Danielle A. Noe © Liturgy Training Publications; photos on pages 3, 12, 15, 17, 27, 29, 32, 35, 55, 57, 81, 87, 88, 94, 96, 108, 109, 112, 116, 130, and 133 by John Zich. Illustrations on page vii © Martin Erspamer; page 10 © Boris Stoilov; and page 103 © Cody F. Miller.

23 22 21 20 19   1 2 3 4 5

Printed in the United States of America

Library of Congress Control Number: 2018968033

ISBN 978-1-61671-346-1

EGCPCS

In memory of
my sister Ruth, and my brother Charlie,
who, in living were a gracious blessing,
and in their suffering and in their dying,
bestowed the enduring grace of the Paschal Mystery
on all of us.

CONTENTS

PREFACE

James sat down, lit a candle, pulled out the parchment, and resumed writing the letter. "Almost done," he said to himself. It was tedious, writing. But his message was important, and he was sending it to all twelve tribes.

Looking at the letter he had received from their representatives, he picked up his quill. "Is anyone among you suffering?" James wrote. "He should pray."[1] Annoyed, glancing back at their letter to him, he mumbled to himself. "They should know these things. Why did they have to ask such elementary questions?"

"Is anyone in good spirits?" James wrote. "He should sing praise."[2] Again, he mumbled to himself. "What else would you expect people to do?" But he restrained himself from adding these editorial comments to the letter he was composing. He knew that such uncharitable thoughts did not come from God.

Just then a knock at the door pulled James away from his meditation. When he opened the door of his home, interior light fell on the saddest face ever.

"Silvanus, what happened?"

"It's Mark. He isn't well."

"He's never well. He's always coughing."

"This time it's different. He's in bed. He can't get up. His voice is weak. His eyes can't focus. He won't eat. We don't know what to do."

James pondered the significance of these new symptoms. "It sounds like what happened to Andronicus."

Silvanus nodded. "Can you come?"

"Yes," said James, "but get Tychicus. We may need both of us."

---

1. See James 5:13.
2. James 5:13.

Silvanus bowed to James, turned, started further down the street, and sought out the other presbyter of the local community. At the door he delivered the same message, and Tychicus immediately came out.

As the two returned to James' house, he joined them up the road to see Mark.

"I have the greatest respect for Mark," said Tychicus. "He has been preparing to write the story of Jesus. He must live to complete the work."

James thought about his own frustrated attempts to write a simple letter. "Mark has gathered many important stories already, including the ones that explain what we are about to do." With that, James showed them the small flask of olive oil he had tucked into his bag. Silvanus smiled.

At Mark's house, the door was already open because of the crowd gathering to see him. James and Tychicus pushed their way in.

Tychicus began to weep. James steadied his shoulders. "Courage. I need you."

Then, James fixed his eyes on the sick man. "Mark!" he commanded.

And Mark turned his face. Their eyes locked. The crowd gasped. "Mark has not responded like that all day," said Silvanus.

Tychicus seized the moment. "Mark, remember the Good News you have learned about Jesus. Remember what his disciples have been telling you, and what you have been telling others: how Jesus first sent out the disciples to continue his ministry of healing. 'They drove out many demons, and they anointed with oil many who were sick and cured them.'"[3]

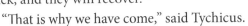

"Remember what the disciples told you about Jesus' last promises," said James. "He told them that they will lay hands on the sick, and they will recover."[4]

"That is why we have come," said Tychicus.

"Let us pray," said James. And everyone knew that "us" was not all of them. It was Tychicus and James.

---

3. Mark 6:13.
4. See Mark 16:18.

Together the two leaders of the community praised God for the gift of Jesus Christ, for the faith that they had received, and for the ministry that they shared. They asked God to forgive Mark's sins, and to strengthen and save him. Then they laid hands on Mark and watched as, immediately, his tense muscles relaxed.

With that, James withdrew the flask of oil and removed the stopper. He poured some on Mark's chest, and, together, he and Tychicus rubbed the oil into the skin of their dear friend. First they anointed the chest, then the arms and the hands, praying all the while. Lovingly, they caressed Mark's face with oil.

"I know that this will help," said Silvanus.

"He will grow strong again," affirmed Tychicus. "He will live to write the Good News."

Tychicus and James left the house and walked back toward their homes. By James' house, they embraced, looked at each other, and separated.

James went back to his writing desk. He was alone and tired, but filled with the Spirit over the events of the past hour. Preparing to be annoyed again, he referenced the letter he had received. But this time it made him smile.

"The sick?" he said aloud, imagining the writers of the letter he had received. "You want to know about the sick?"

Sensing the presence of the Holy Spirit who had guided him throughout this evening, James picked up his quill.

"Is anyone among you sick? He should summon the presbyters of the Church, and they should pray over him and anoint [him] with oil in the name of the Lord, and the prayer of faith will save the sick person, and the Lord will raise him up. If he has committed any sins, he will be forgiven."[5]

With that, James set down his quill, mumbling once more. "Will anyone really read this? Will anyone pay attention? Will anyone care for the sick?"

Setting his parchment aside, praying again for his friend, James blew out the candle and shuffled off to bed.

—Paul Turner

PAUL TURNER is pastor of the Cathedral of the Immaculate Conception in Kansas City, Missouri, and director of the Office of Divine Worship for the Diocese of Kansas City–St. Joseph. He holds a doctorate in sacred theology from Sant'Anselmo in Rome and has published many pastoral resources.

---

5. Mark 6:13.

WELCOME

Welcome to this *Guide for Celebrating the Pastoral Care of the Sick*. Suffering and illness have always been among the greatest problems that trouble the human spirit. Christians feel and experience pain as do all other people; yet their faith helps them to grasp more deeply the mystery of suffering and to bear their pain with greater courage.[1]

The Catholic Church has a long-standing and worthy tradition of taking care of her sick members. Indeed, this ministry is rooted in the ministry of Jesus himself who told his disciples that he did not come to heal those who are well, but those who are sick.[2] It was this ministry that Jesus gave to his disciples when he commissioned them to "cure the sick, raise the dead, cleanse lepers, drive out demons."[3] In the Letter of James we find evidence that a simple ritual had developed in the early period of the Christian community.[4] The elements of the ritual included the prayers of the elders and the community, an anointing with oil, and forgiveness of sins. In the course of the Church's history this rite has changed in many ways; yet the primary elements of the ritual celebration have remained constant. The intent of the Church's ministry has always been to express the loving mercy of God; to strengthen the faith of those who are sick; to assure the sick of the solicitude of their brothers and sisters in faith; to give the sick hope in the love of the Lord; and to celebrate the power of the Risen Lord over the limitations of human suffering and illness.

About This Book

This book is intended to assist pastors, presiders, pastoral and worship teams, deacons, ministers of care, extraordinary ministers of Holy Communion, music ministers, and liturgy coordinators with a comprehensive overview of

---

1. See *Pastoral Care of the Sick: Rites of Anointing and Viaticum* (PCS), 1.
2. See Mark 2:17.
3. Matthew 10:8.
4. See James 5:13–15.

the various rites and a deeper understanding of the sacraments of healing. Those who are engaged in health care roles, relatives of the persons who are sick, as well as members of the parish community will also discover new insights to help them participate in this work of the Church, and in the often difficult moment in the life of a family member or a brother or sister in faith.

This book offers a brief overview of the history of the liturgical rites and the theology of the sacraments of healing as both of these aspects evolved throughout the life of the Church. This exploration of the development of the sacraments will afford a deeper understanding of the elements of the sacraments and a better appreciation of what we do and why.

There are several rites within the larger framework of *Pastoral Care of the Sick: Rites of Anointing and Viaticum* which address the numerous pastoral situations found in the life of a community of faith. Each of these rites will be explored and discussed in some detail, with a view to understanding the richness of the sacrament as a liturgical celebration both for the person who is sick and the larger community of the faithful. Each of the rites has a number of options that can be used depending on the circumstances of the sick person, the place where the sick person is, as well as other pastoral considerations.

This resource includes a section providing answers to frequently asked questions in this ministry. An annotated bibliography of resources available for those who might choose to do further reading and research on these rites is also included. The annotated bibliography will be a wonderful resource for those who prepare for the celebration of the rites, both with an individual and with the parish community, catechists, and those who are involved with the Rite of Christian Initiation of Adults. The glossary offers a helpful guide to the words and phrases associated with these rites.

My hope is that readers of this book will discover new insights regarding the rites of the sick; come to a new appreciation of the healing power of God in our lives; know again the importance of our ministry to those who are sick; and be renewed in their concern for those whom they accompany in their suffering and illness. Those who are sick may also benefit from a realization that they bear witness to the Paschal Mystery of Jesus Christ.

About the Author

J. PHILIP (PHIL) HORRIGAN is a priest of the Archdiocese of Kingston, Ontario. He holds master's degrees in education and theology, and a doctor of ministry from Catholic Theological Union (CTU) in Chicago. He is an adjunct professor in the Word and Worship department at CTU.

Phil has spent over fifty years in pastoral ministry in Canada and the US. From 1997 until 2009 he was the director of the Department of Art and Architecture at the Office for Divine Worship, Archdiocese of Chicago. He is now an independent liturgical design consultant and a frequent presenter and author on various issues related to the building and renovation of churches and the liturgical environment; on the history and components of liturgical design; and on sacramental theology, the spiritual and ecclesial dimensions of liturgical ministries, and the pastoral implications of liturgical rituals, documents, and praxis. His particular interest is exploring the relationship between ritual space and ritual event.

Phil has contributed to many resources published by Liturgy Training Publications including *Sourcebook for Sundays, Seasons, and Weekdays*; *Pastoral Liturgy* magazine; *Rite* magazine; *At Home with the Word*; *The Liturgy Documents, Volume I: Essential Documents for Parish Worship*, 5th ed.; *The Liturgy Documents, Volume IV: Supplemental Documents for Parish Worship, Devotions, Formation, and Catechesis*; *To Crown the Year: Decorating the Church through the Seasons*, 2nd ed.; *A Pastoral Commentary on Sacrosanctum Concilium, The Constitution on the Sacred Liturgy of the Second Vatican Council,* chapter IV, "Sacred Art and Sacred Furnishings"; and has authored *Guide for Celebrating Reconciliation*, a companion book in the Preparing Parish Worship series.

The Theological and Historical Developments of the Anointing of the Sick

"Christ, who during his life often visited and healed the sick,
loves them in their illness."

—*Pastoral Care of the Sick: Rites of Anointing and Viaticum*, 1

There are three distinct and interrelated elements in the celebration of the Anointing of the Sick: the prayer of faith, the laying on of hands, and the anointing with oil. Each of these elements has its own meaning and each has a particular historical genesis and development. The convergence of these three parts into a ritual format has some precedence in the Old Testament world of the people of God. As we shall see in exploring the Christian tradition these same three elements shape the liturgical experience of the early Church and provide the basis of the liturgy of anointing that the Church celebrates to this day.

The Mediterranean World of the Old Testament

In the domestic culture of the Mediterranean world, oil was a common item as well as a prized commodity in the market place. It was used for illumination in lamps, cooking and eating, a cleansing substance for bathing, and for medicinal uses. In the area of commerce it was bought and sold as a cosmetic.

There are numerous references to the use of oil in the ritual life of the Israelites. The pouring of oil on a person or object usually meant that the person or object was set aside for a particular purpose. Thus, the action of being anointed carried with it a commission, as in the case of the anointing of a king; or the designation for special use, as with the objects set aside for worship. When Samuel anointed Saul as king he took a "flask he had with him, Samuel poured oil on Saul's head and kissed him, saying: 'The LORD anoints you ruler over his people Israel.'"[1] The action of Samuel was regarded as the action of God working through his servant and conveying to Saul a divine appointment. The gesture and the oil are vehicles of the will of God, and the assignment for Saul is to do God's work. In Psalm 89, the psalmist places these words in the mouth of the Lord: "I have chosen David, my servant; / with my holy oil I have anointed him."[2] In this text we note that the act of anointing is attributed to the Lord's own doing. The earthly element of oil carries a divine intent: the bestowal of a commission, along with the grace and power of the Lord to fulfil its purpose.

———— ●● ————

The Spirit of the Lord is upon me,
because he has anointed me
to bring glad tidings to the poor.
He has sent me to proclaim liberty
    to captives
and recovery of sight to the blind,
to let the oppressed go free,
and to proclaim a year acceptable to
    the Lord.

—Luke 4:18–19

In the Book of Isaiah we read this familiar passage: "The spirit of the Lord GOD is upon me, / because the LORD has anointed me; / He has sent me to bring good news to the afflicted, / to bind up the brokenhearted, / To proclaim liberty to captives, / release to the prisoners."[3] This is the text that Jesus reads from the scroll of Isaiah in the synagogue at Nazareth.[4] For Luke, this marks the beginning of Jesus' public ministry, a ministry that he accepts from God and that will shape his actions and his teaching. Other examples of the anointing of persons include the ordination of the sons of Aaron as priests[5] and the installation of the prophet Elisha.[6]

The anointing of objects with oil is also seen as a consecration, meaning that the item is designated for a particular purpose within the context of a human divine event. The wonderful story of Jacob's dream describes him anointing the stone that he had put under his head. He set the stone on a pillar, forming a kind of altar, and "poured oil on top of it."[7] Jacob then makes

---

1. 1 Samuel 10:1a; see also, 1 Samuel 15:1.
2. Psalm 89:21.
3. Isaiah 61:1–2.
4. See Luke 4:16–19.
5. See Exodus 28:40–41. A more elaborate ceremony is described in 29:1–9.
6. See 1 Kings 19:16.
7. Genesis 28:18.

Throughout the Judeo-Christian tradition, oil has been used for sacred rites for particular purposes.

a vow to the Lord, an indication that he has been changed by this experience and that he will place his life at the service of the Lord.

The author of the Book of Exodus describes in amazing detail the recipe for "a sacred anointing oil" that is to be used to anoint "the tent of meeting and the ark of the covenant, the table and all its utensils, the menorah and its utensils, the altar of incense and the altar for burnt offerings with all its utensils, and the basin with its stand." Then this instruction is added, "When you have consecrated them, they shall be most sacred; whatever touches them shall be sacred. . . . Tell the Israelites: As sacred anointing oil this shall belong to me throughout your generations. It may not be used in any ordinary anointing of the body, nor may you make any other oil of a like mixture. It is sacred, and shall be treated as sacred by you."[8]

There are some aspects of this elaborate ritual that will appear in the Christian tradition. The blessing and use of a particular oil for religious purposes, the sense of holiness that is conveyed by the gesture of anointing of persons and objects, and the belief that the ritual itself places those who participate in it in the company of the Lord.

8. Exodus 30:22–32.

> Then, dipping his right finger in the oil on his left palm, [the priest] shall sprinkle some of it with his finger seven times before the LORD.
>
> —Leviticus 14:16

A reference to the use of oil that is closer to the Catholic treatment of the Anointing of the Sick appears in Leviticus.[9] The priest is instructed to use oil as part of a ceremony for the cleansing of a person with leprosy. The oil, which is specially prepared, is to be applied to several parts of the body. In keeping with the religious understanding of that time, namely that such sickness is related to sinfulness, sacrificial offerings are made before God. Another interesting reference in this passage is the connection between illness as a result of sin and as a punishment for sin. This theology will surface in the Christian tradition generations later.[10]

Two other references deserve mentioning here. Anointing with oil was a form of hospitality. In Psalm 23, the actions of the Lord are considered a gesture of friendship and a sign that the Lord cares: "You set a table before me / in front of my enemies; / You anoint my head with oil; / my cup overflows."[11] Closely related to the sign of hospitality is that of gladness and refreshment. The psalmist sings of the Lord who "bring[s] forth food from the earth, / wine to gladden the heart, / oil to make the face shine, / and bread to sustain the human heart."[12] The oracle of Isaiah echoes this same sentiment when he proclaims, "The spirit of the Lord GOD is upon me / . . . / to place on those who mourn in Zion / a diadem instead of ashes, / To give them oil of gladness instead of mourning, / a glorious mantle instead of a faint spirit."[13]

These aspects of anointing persons will find their way into the rituals of the early Christian tradition and eventually in the evolving ritual patterns and understanding of the Catholic Church: the laying on of hands; the pouring of oil on a person, usually on the head; the special honor given to the oil itself, even though it is a common domestic item; and the understanding that the ritual is a vehicle and sign of God's appointment and commissioning of one made holy to do a holy thing.

---

9. See Leviticus 14:15–18.

10. Later in this book we will see that the anointing of parts of the body is part of the sacramental rite of Anointing of the Sick. The element of touch has thus a long tradition in the various rites of healing.

11. Psalm 23:5.

12. Psalm 104:14c–15.

13. Isaiah 61:1, 3.

The Ministry of Jesus

The healing ministry of Jesus was extensive, compassionate, and inclusive. As Jesus made his away across the land of Judea he brought the healing power of God into the lives of those he encountered wherever he found them—in the synagogue, in private homes, in the marketplace, and even as he was walking along from one place to another. In the four accounts of the Gospel there are over fifty recorded instances where Jesus heals someone of an illness, disability, or demonic possession. Although some of these are repeated accounts, the sheer number of recorded incidents by the four evangelists is clear testimony to Jesus' desire to fulfil the words of Isaiah addressed to the Suffering Servant: "Yet it was our pain that he bore, / our sufferings he endured"[14] In fact, Matthew includes this reference in his comment on Jesus' healing of Peter's mother-in-law. For Matthew, the healing ministry of Jesus was "to fulfil what had been said by Isaiah the prophet."[15]

The healing ministry of Jesus was the restoration of wholeness and the manifestation of the intervention of God in human affairs; most especially in situations of illness, suffering, and brokenness. In many of the encounters between Jesus and those

> "Daughter, your faith has saved you. Go in peace and be cured of your affliction."
>
> —Mark 5:34

he healed, he broke through the social, religious, and economic barriers and conventions of his time. He extended the astonishing mercy of God to those who were poor (in the healing of the woman with the hemorrhage who had spent all her savings[16]); those who were ostracized because of their illness (like the person with leprosy[17]); and those whose infirmity was considered a punishment for sin (as with the man born blind[18]). Jesus healed on the Sabbath in the synagogue, which was a transgression of the law of the Sabbath and an affront to the religious leaders.[19] In his healing actions he often touched those who were ill, a gesture that was forbidden by the laws of purity; and he expelled demons, an action that was understood to be reserved for God alone.

---

14. Isaiah 53:4.
15. Matthew 8:17.
16. See Mark 5:25–35.
17. See Mark 1:40–42; Luke 5:12–16, Matthew 8:1–4.
18. See John 9:1–41.
19. See Luke 13:10–17.

I sought the LORD, and he answered me,
delivered me from all my fears.
Look to him and be radiant,
and your faces may not blush for shame.
This poor one cried out and the LORD heard,
and from all his distress he saved him.

—Psalm 34:5–7

It is ironic that in many ways the healing ministry of Jesus not only led to continued tensions between him and the religious leaders, but also contributed to the evidence brought against him that led to his Crucifixion. The synagogue was regarded as the conventional place where the religious leaders taught the Law of Moses, and provided healing; in other words the place for preaching God's Word and doing God's work. When Jesus usurps their role and presents himself as coming from God and doing God's work, it was inevitable that there would be clashes with the Scribes and the Pharisees. After he restores the withered hand of a man in the synagogue on the Sabbath, Matthew notes that "the Pharisees went out and took counsel against him to put him to death."[20]

The reaction of the people to the healing acts of Jesus was quite different, from awe to suspicion.[21] These varied reactions tell us that the healing ministry of Jesus was accepted by the people as a sign of God's providence and an indication that God had not forgotten them. God really did hear the cry of the poor. In many situations, the joyful announcement of a healing by the recipient led to faith for those who heard the Good News. Those who had been scorned or dismissed from both social and religious circles became evangelizers. These people were unlikely bearers of the astonishing mercy of God. Then there were those who saw in Jesus a prophet and the personification of the long awaited Messiah. They rejoiced that the day of the Lord had arrived in their midst; indeed, they had never seen anything quite like the things he did or heard from anyone else the "gracious words that came from his mouth."[22]

One of the questions that arises from Jesus' healing ministry is whether his intervention is a physical healing, a spiritual healing, or both. This question is discussed by Scripture scholars and theologians to this day. The incident that gives rise to this issue is the healing of the paralyzed man. The man is placed before Jesus by his friends who let him down through the roof of

---

20.   Matthew 12:14.

21.   See especially, Matthew 9:8; Matthew 14:35–36; Matthew 15:30–31; Mark 2:12b; Mark 6:56; Mark 7:37; Luke 4:36–37; Luke 5:26; Luke 7:16; Luke 9:42b–43.

22.   Luke 4:22.

the house.[23] In response to the apparent faith of the friends of the paralytic, Jesus pronounces forgiveness for his sins. This causes the scribes to question how Jesus has the authority forgive sins, since no one can forgive sins except for God. To add to the controversy, Jesus asks the scribes what is easier to say to the paralytic, "Your sins are forgiven"[24] or "Rise, take up your mat, and walk?"[25] And then Jesus tells him to take his mat and go home. Both the forgiveness of the man's sins, whether by Jesus or by God through Jesus, and the healing of the man's paralysis, are interventions of God. The fact that they occur in the same story to the same person gives rise to the question noted above. Jesus doesn't give any indication that the two are integrally related; that is to say, his paralysis is not the result of his sins, though that was a common thinking of the time. This thinking is referenced in the story of the healing of the man born blind in John 9:1–41. When the disciples ask, "Rabbi, who sinned, this man or his parents, that he was born blind?" Jesus responds, "Neither he nor his parents sinned; it is so that the works of God might be made visible through him."[26]

The forgiveness of the paralyzed man's sins and his physical healing are direct signs of divine activity and represent the power and the desire of God to heal both body and spirit. Jesus is the vehicle of God's compassion, one that restores the human condition to wholeness and at the same leads those of faith to give glory to God. "They were all astounded and glorified God, saying, 'We have never seen anything like this.'"[27]

By way of a contemporary comment on this story, it is true that sin can "paralyze" our spiritual well-being; but not every moment of spiritual healing and forgiveness brings about a physical restoration. Nonetheless, like the friends of the paralyzed man, we present ourselves to the Lord when we are ill and trust that the Lord will provide what is restorative and compassionate.

There are three incidents of anointing in the Gospel accounts. One involves the anointing of the body of Jesus in the tomb by a group of women.[28] The anointing of a corpse with aromatic spices had the practical

---

23. See Mark 2:2–12 and Matthew 9:2–7.
24. Luke 7:48.
25. John 5:8.
26. John 9:1–4
27. Mark 2:12b. For an excellent commentary on this passage see John R. Donahue, SJ, and Daniel J. Harrington, SJ, *The Gospel of Mark, Sacra Pagina Series*, vol. 2 (Collegeville, MN: Liturgical Press, 2002).
28. See Mark 16:1 and Luke 24:1.

> He approached the victim, poured oil and wine over his wounds and bandaged them.
>
> —Luke 10:3

effect of minimizing the odor associated with human remains. It was also a way of honoring the dead.

The second reference to anointing occurs in the apostolic ministry of the Twelve after Jesus sends them out to extend his own ministry of teaching and healing. And so they went out "two by two and [Jesus] gave them authority over unclean spirits."[29] Mark's reference to the anointing with oil might reflect a practice that was already in place in the Markan community. This ministry of the Twelve anticipates the ecclesial commission that Jesus will bestow on all his disciples at the end of his public mission, a commission that shapes the ministry of the Church to this day. A third reference to anointing occurs in the parable of the Good Samaritan.[30] In this incident, the Samaritan pours oil and wine on the wounds of the person who has been mugged by robbers. The use of oil in this instance is medicinal and serves to underline the compassion of the Samaritan as well as emphasizing the message of the parable.

The Early Church

The disciples of Jesus shared in his ministry of healing both during his time with them and in their own ministry after the Resurrection. Jesus' commission to the disciples was very clear as Luke reports: Jesus called the Twelve together and gave them power and authority over all demons as well as to cure diseases. Jesus sent out the disciples to proclaim the Kingdom of God and to heal.[31] In his first letter to the Corinthians, St. Paul speaks of the variety of gifts that shape the life of the Church of Corinth. Among those gifts, which come from the Spirit, is the gift of healing.[32] Paul doesn't record any particular example or ritual of healing, only that it was one of the charisms that the Christian community possessed; presumably it was a practice that he was aware of.

There are, however, several incidents of healing recorded in the Acts of the Apostles. Two of these accounts are by St. Peter, who, along with St. John, take up the mandate of Jesus and spread the Good News of the Risen Lord

---

29. Mark 6:7.
30. See Luke 10:29–37.
31. See Luke 9:1–2.
32. See 1 Corinthians 12:9.

throughout the region. In the first incident, they encounter a man who had been lame form birth and who was begging in the Temple area. The lame man asks Peter and John for alms, but Peter replies, "I have neither silver nor gold, but what I do have I

> There are different kinds of spiritual gifts but the same Spirit . . . to another gifts of healing by the same Spirit.
>
> —1 Corinthians 12:4, 9

give you; in the name of Jesus Christ the Nazorean, [rise and] walk."[33] The healing of this person echoes the mission of Jesus who said that he was sent make the lame walk[34]; the reaction of the one who was healed is similar to those whom Jesus healed. Healing leads to praise of God. Peter makes it clear that he acts in the name of "Jesus Christ the Nazorean,"[35] thus, indicating that he does not act on his own accord, but only as a vehicle of the power and mercy of the Risen Lord. There is no mention of any ritual in this story, only that Peter took the man's hand and raised him up. This is resurrection language, and a sign that the power of the Risen Lord flows through the Apostle Peter and gives witness to the words of Jesus who told his disciples that they would do the works that he has done.[36]

In the town of Lydda, Peter meets Aeneas who had been paralyzed for eight years. Once again, Peter invokes the name of the Lord, saying to Aeneas, "Jesus Christ heals you. Get up and make your bed."[37] There is no explanation why Peter thought that Aeneas should immediately make his bed. Perhaps it was to show that being healed allowed one to return to their normal life; in other words, to be made whole again by the power of the Lord. The account concludes by saying that the people who witnessed this healing "turned to the Lord."[38] Again, the person who is healed becomes a witness to others; he is a new disciple who, through his healing, leads others to faith.

One additional healing from Acts of the Apostles is worth noting. It occurs during the missionary journey of Paul to the island of Malta. Paul is welcomed into the house of Publius, "the chief of the island"[39] whose father is ill. The author of Acts reports that "Paul visited him and, after praying,

---

33. Acts 3:6.
34. See Matthew 11:5.
35. Acts 3:6.
36. See Mark 16:18b.
37. Acts 9:34.
38. Acts 9:35.
39. Acts 28:7.

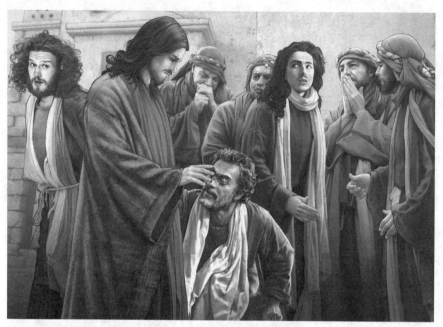

"The prayer of faith will save the sick person, and the Lord will raise him up" (James 5:15).

laid his hands on him and healed him."[40] Paul's action of praying and the laying on of hands in a simple ritual offers precedence for a future rite that will include these key elements in the sacramental rite of the Anointing of the Sick. Note that there is no mention of the use of oil in these three healings. That changes with the description of a healing recorded in the Letter of James.

The preeminent text from the New Testament that forms the biblical foundation for the Anointing of the Sick appears in the letter of James:

> Is anyone among you suffering? He should pray. Is anyone in good spirits? He should sing praise. Is anyone among you sick? He should summon the presbyters of the church, and they should pray over [him] and anoint him with oil in the name of the Lord, and the prayer of faith will save the sick person, and the Lord will raise him up. If he has committed any sins, he will be forgiven.[41]

Because this text figures prominently in the subsequent practice of the Church and influences the theology associated with the eventual naming of this ritual action as a sacrament, it warrants a brief commentary here.

---

40. Acts 28:8.
41. James 5:13–15.

The repetition of the phrase "among you" situates the healing action within the ecclesial community. The believing community provides the context for concern for the person who suffers or who is ill. It is the prayer of the faithful that is an integral part of the rite that is described. There is no existing evidence what the prayer or prayers might have been; only that it was deemed important that prayers be said by the person who was suffering and/or sick and by the members of the Church. The actual condition of the sick person is not described in any detail; though if he or she is able to call for the elders it can be assumed that they are not in danger of death.

The elders of the Church would have been the appointed leaders of the community, in particular those who held some responsibility for the liturgical services that were celebrated in the early Church. The term does not refer to their age but to their association with the apostolic ministry. It seems premature to associate them with any kind of hierarchy, or even to assume that they were male, although that is probably the case.

There are two elements to this simple ritual action: praying over the sick person and an anointing with oil. The sentence structure seems to indicate that it is only the elders who pray; but the overall tone of the letter indicates that it is the larger community of believers who are included in this exhortation and hence would be present and joining in the "prayer of faith."[42] It is this prayer of faith that will save the sick person, an indication that this is not a medical healing but a spiritual healing. The person will be saved; he or she will be raised up in the Lord and by the Lord. This is the language of resurrection, not resuscitation. Just as the Lord was raised from the dead by God, so the sick will be raised up by the Lord through the ministry of the Church that assembles and prays in the name of the Risen Lord.

The text continues with the assertion that if the person has sinned their sins will be forgiven. Unlike the earlier accounts of healing by Jesus, where some assumed that the person was sick as a result of sin, this is not the implication here. The person in question in the letter of James is forgiven if he or she has committed any sin. Thus, the whole person is restored; being healed of their infirmity and saved from sin is what God does. Recall the story of Jesus' healing and forgiving the paralyzed man.[43]

Those who gather with the sick person are asked to pray *over* and not just *for* the person who is sick. This gesture means that those who are

---

42. James 5:15.
43. See Mark 2:1–12.

Those who gather with the sick are to pray over the person who is ill.

gathered are more directly engaged in the healing, and that the posture of praying over the sick person is more expressive of the responsibility of the faithful than simply praying for the person.

The directive to anoint the sick person with oil is likely indicative of an existing practice in the Church or Churches addressed by the author of this letter. This is the only account in the New Testament where the anointing with oil and the prayer of faithful are combined with a healing from sickness and the forgiveness of sin.

This seminal text was influential in the development of the Rite of the Anointing the Sick from the early Church until the present day. Further, it expresses a number of aspects of an ecclesiology associated with the sacraments. First, it is the responsibility of the faithful to continue the healing ministry of Jesus and to do so by actively caring for those who suffer and those who are sick. Second, the community of faith is to be engaged in a ritual praying over the sick person; their presence is an important part of the healing process. Third, the liturgical leadership in the Church has a significant role to play in the ministry of healing.

The theological implications of this text also influenced the Church's understanding of the Sacrament of the Anointing of the Sick. First, it is the intervention of God that brings about spiritual healing and forgiveness of sin. Second, faith is the context for the healing action of God, and the faith community is the *locus* for the salvific action of God through the Risen Lord. Third, the human condition of suffering and sickness is not in itself terminal; hope for those who suffer or are sick is found in the merciful love of God.

These various elements found their way in and out of the history of the rite, with different emphasis, as the Church's practice and understanding developed over the following centuries. They became even more pronounced in the reformed Rite of the Anointing of the Sick: *Pastoral Care of the Sick: Rites of Anointing and Viaticum* (1972).

The First Eight Hundred Years

After the apostolic era, the practice of Christian healing continued but the evidence of how and when it was done is fragmented. However, sources suggest that there was a healing ministry in the Church although the emphasis was centered more on the oil itself and less on how it was used in a ritual. In fact, there is no existing evidence of a set ritual for anointing until the ninth century. One of the earliest texts that refers to the Anointing of the Sick is in a prayer of blessing of the oil found in the Apostolic Tradition of Hippolytus (c. 215):

"If anyone offers oil, he [the bishop] shall make Eucharist [render thanks] as at the oblation of the bread and wine. But he shall not say word for word [the same prayer] but with similar effect saying, God who sanctifies this oil, as Thou dost grant unto all who are anointed and receive of it the hallowing wherewith Thou didst anoint kings, priests and prophets, so [grant that] it may give strength to all who taste of it and health to all who use it."[44]

This liturgical prayer indicates that the bishop blessed the oil during the celebration of the Eucharist and the oil was presented by the faithful in the same manner as the bread and wine. The prayer is a form of epiclesis, an invocation of the favor of God for the purpose of sanctifying the oil. Once blessed the oil is capable of producing the healing effects for those who use it. In his commentary on this text, Charles Gusmer notes that the oil can be consumed by the person who is sick, or applied externally.[45] There is no indication that ordained ministers or other ministers of the Church did the anointing.

Another prayer of blessing that is thought to date from the fifth century and is found in both the Gelasian and Gregorian sacramentaries has a similar tone:

"Send down from heaven, we beseech Thee, Lord, the Holy Spirit, the Paraclete, upon the richness of this oil, which Thou has designed to bring forth from the green tree for refreshment of mind and body. And may Thy blessing be to all who anoint, taste, and touch, a protection for body, soul, and spirit, for dispelling all sufferings, all sickness, all illness of mind and body. With this oil Thou didst anoint priests, kings, prophets and martyrs; Thy perfect chrism, blessed by Thee, O Lord, and remaining within our

---

44. Gregory Dix, ed., *The Apostoloc Tradition* (London: SPCK, 1968), 10.
45. See Charles Gusmer, *And You Visited Me: Sacramental Ministry to the Sick and Dying* (Collegeville, MN: Liturgical Press, 1990), 12.

inner organs, in the name of our Lord Jesus Christ. Through whom all these good gifts, O Lord, thou dost ever create."[46]

The wording of this prayer reveals that the manner of using the oil is by tasting, touching, and applying or anointing. The stated intention in the use of the oil is extensive: "a protection of body, soul, and spirit." The efficacy of the oil comes from the work of the Holy Spirit in an element of God's creation, "the green tree," thus placing the source of spiritual and bodily well-being in the hands of God.

Another source from this period that underlines the practice and the theology of anointing is found in the writings of Pope Innocent I (416). In a letter to one of his bishops he states:

- The words from the letter of James refer to the faithful who are sick and who can be anointed.

- The oil is prepared by the bishop and not only priests but all Christians may use it for anointing themselves or their family.

- Only the faithful in good standing can be anointed; thus excluding penitents and catechumens.[47]

The leader of the Church in Gall, Caesarius of Arles (d. 543) encouraged lay anointings and refers to the practice of anointing in the Church by priests. He states:

"That as often as one is taken by sickness, let him (sic) get to church and receive the body and blood of Christ and be anointed by the priests with blessed oil. Let them ask the priests and deacons to pray over them in Christ's name, which will bring them both health of body and the remission of sins, for the Lord has been pleased to promise this through his Apostle James."[48]

These conclusions can be drawn from these sources pertaining to the development of the ritual practice of anointing and the theological understanding associated with it:

- The blessing of the oil by the bishop is an important part of the larger ritual action. The oil is referred to as sacred oil, blessed oil, holy oil, and prepared oil.

---

46. Paul F. Palmer, ed., *Sacraments and Forgiveness, Sources of Christian Theology II* (Westminster, MD: Newman Press, 1959), 88.

47. See Gusmer, 15.

48. Gusmer, 16.

- The efficacy of the oil is related to its being blessed; there is an analogy to the waters of Baptism and to the invocation of the Holy Spirit, an epiclesis, over the created element that it may become a vehicle of divine power.

- While the preparation and blessing of the oil seems to have been reserved to the bishop, the actual anointing could be done by anyone, including a self-application by the person who was sick.

- Although there were prayers for blessing the oil, there is no existing text from this time for its application; although it might be assumed that some prayers, either fixed or spontaneous, accompanied the anointing.

Today, a person who is sick can be anointed more than once.

It isn't until the beginning of the ninth century that a formula for anointing appears.

- The person who is sick can be anointed more than once. The nature of the illness is not restricted; almost every form of infirmity is included in the reference to "body, soul, and spirit." A prayer by an Eastern bishop, Serapion of Thumis, includes a list of issues that anointing can address: every disease and every sickness; every demon and every unclean spirit; banishing all fever, all chill, and all weariness; a means of grace and goodness and the remission of sins; a medicament of life and salvation, unto health and soundness of soul and body and spirit, unto perfect well-being.[49]

- During this time there is no mention of anointing as being a preparation for death.[50]

- The assertion that the forgiveness or remission of sins is one of the results of anointing is not yet a developed theology. The connection

49. Gusmer, 13.
50. Gusmer, 13.

between forgiveness of sin and anointing will continue to be debated by scholars until the present day and the Sacraments of Reconciliation and Anointing will find their way into the present rite of anointing.

- There was a clear indication that the ecclesial community had a role in the healing ministry. They were encouraged to accompany the sick person to the church; if the person was not able to be present before the bishops or the priests, then members of the faithful could take the blessed oil to the home of the sick. It is quite likely that the faithful who gathered either in the church or in the home would have engaged in the "prayer of faith" that had its beginnings in the time of James the Apostle.

- The prayers of blessing the oil and the actual anointing speak of the restoration of both bodily and spiritual health. In subsequent developments an ongoing discussion will arise about whether anointing effects a physical change or a spiritual one, or both.

The Carolingian Reforms

The liturgical reforms in this period of Church history, often referred to as the time of the Franco-Roman liturgy, were especially significant within the overall liturgical life of the Church. This work is not the place for a survey of those changes, but a couple of the broader developments relate to the Anointing of the Sick. This period saw the increasing prominence of the ordained in the celebration of the liturgy. This led to a shift from the more communal nature of the liturgy to one that saw an increasing dominance of the ordained in dictating the ritual patterns and their role as the primary celebrant in the liturgy to the exclusion of the faithful's participation. Also, during this period there was an effort to gather the various prayers of the liturgical rites into sacramentaries, a compilation of prayers into a single book for the sole use by the bishop or priest who presided over the liturgical action.

It is from this period that we find a full ritual text for the Anointing of the Sick. It is the oldest extant ritual available.[51] The prayers of the Rite of Anointing reveal some interesting developments. From the Mozarabic source we read: "And let him [bishop or priest] anoint the sick man with sanctified oil, making signs of the cross on the back [of the neck] and on the throat,

---

51. Gusmer, 21–2.

between the shoulders and on the breast; or let him anoint further the place where the pain is more pronounced."[52] The rubrics direct that the sick person should receive the Body and Blood of the Lord, noting that if the person is in sin, the sins are forgiven.[53]

Another reference from the same source appears to describe an existing practice that sounds very much like the gesture used in the current rite: "Now many priests anoint the sick also on the five senses, that is, on the eyelids, and on the inner nostrils and on the tip of the nose or externally, and on the outside of the lips and on the outside or back of the hands. Accordingly, on all these members let them make the sign of the cross with sacred oil, saying; In the name of the Father and of the Son, and of the Holy Spirit."[54]

We also begin to see the celebration of the Sacrament of Penance along with sacramental anointing. By the year 800, the practice of death-bed confession, along with the disappearance of the public penitential discipline that originated in the early Church, was widespread. Since it was believed that anointing with blessed oil also forgave the sins of the sick person, it became customary for anointing to take place as part of the confession when one was near death. Since only a priest or bishop could absolve, then only a priest or bishop could now anoint. By the twelfth century the order of these sacraments changed from Penance, Anointing, and Viaticum to Penance, Viaticum, and Anointing. Anointing was now associated with preparation for dying instead of a return to health.[55]

With the decline of the public Rite of Penance, known as canonical penance, private confession, which was repeatable, became the norm.

No longer the last sacrament, the Sacrament of Anointing was restored by the Second Vatican Council as a sacrament of healing.

52.   Gusmer states that during the Carolingian Reform (AD 815–845) a compilation of sources from the Roman, Gallican, and Mozarabic rites informed the rite of anointing. The rubric noted above appears to be from the Mozarabic source. See H.B. Porter, "The Origin of the Medieval Rite for Anointing the Sick or Dying," *Journal of Theological Studies* 7 (1956): 211–25.

53.   Gusmer, 23.

54.   Gusmer, 24.

55.   Gusmer, 26.

Subsequently, the prayers associated with a death-bed confession migrated to the Rite of Anointing. Anointing now had a more penitential character and the emphasis was on the remission of sin instead of an expected recovery from sickness. The prayers for healing were gradually dropped and replaced by those that spoke of the remission of sin and the hope of eternal salvation.[56] This last anointing, or *extrema unctio* led to the name Extreme Unction, a name that was maintained until the liturgical reform of the Second Vatican Council (1962–65).

An unfortunate and scandalous practice developed during this period where three or more priests were included for an anointing service, and a stipend was demanded for each of them. This practice, along with other liturgical abuses, was attacked by the reformers in the sixteenth century.

The Scholastic Period

The Scholastic period, which spanned the Middle Ages, was a time of great theological scholarship in the Church. The Dominicans, led by Thomas Aquinas and Albert the Great, and the Franciscans, with Bonaventure and Duns Scotus, were the leading schoolmen during this period. A number of issues related to Anointing of the Sick were debated by these respective schools of thought. They disagreed on the effects of anointing, questioning whether it brought healing for the person who was sick or was a preparation for death. The Franciscans held that Anointing remitted venial sins since Reconciliation remitted mortal sins. The Dominicans maintained that anointing remitted the remnants of sin which remained even after forgiveness. Thomas Aquinas maintained that only secondarily did the sacrament effect physical healing, but it always offered the grace of God.

Both schools of thought agreed that the sacrament was preparation for final glory and entrance into heaven. Aquinas also believed that the Anointing of the Sick could effect physical healing if the disease was the result of sinful habits which lingered in a person's soul after the sins were committed. Also, anointing could remit unconfessed sins if the sick person cooperated with the grace of the sacrament.

The results of the scholarship during this era shaped the sacramental practice and theology of the Church for the next several centuries. In

---

56. Joseph Martos, *Doors to the Sacred: A Historical Introduction to the Sacraments in the Catholic Church*, rev. ed. (Liguori, MS: Liguori/Triumph, 2001), 335.

practice, the rite itself had been simplified and it was more available to the faithful, since only one priest was needed for an anointing. However, since anointing was intended for those who were near death, those who were sick but not in danger of death no longer presented themselves for anointing. The prayers asking for physical healing were not included in the simplified rite and the prayer that accompanied the actual anointing of the senses was penitential: "Through this holy anointing and his tender mercy, may the Lord forgive whatever sins you have committed by sight, by hearing,"[57] and so forth as the oil was signed on the various parts of the body. This prayer made its way into the Roman sacramentary where it remained until the reformed rite following the Second Vatican Council (1962–65).

The theologians of the Middle Ages sought to define and explain the existing practice of anointing the sick through the lens of the ministry of the ordained and the sacrament of orders. As a result it became more and more isolated from the community's participation and hence from the notion that it was part of the broader healing ministry of the Church. Both Bonaventure and Aquinas had held that the sacrament should never be given to those who were healthy. Aquinas added that it should not be given to people who might recover from illness lest the purpose of the sacrament be thwarted. It should only be given when death was imminent—to those who were on their way to the next life.[58] Master Herman (d. 1160), a disciple of Peter Abelard, stated that "Every Christian is anointed three times: first for his inception, namely in baptism; secondly, in confirmation, where the gifts of grace are conferred; thirdly, on departing (*in exitu*), where if sins are present, they are remitted in whole or in part."[59]

One of the issues that concerned theologians after the scholarship of Aquinas and Bonaventure was whether a person who was seriously ill or unconscious could be anointed. The understanding was that since the sacrament was the mysterious work of God, a person's awareness was not required as long as their soul was disposed to receiving God's grace.[60] This thinking separated the spiritual being, the soul, from the physical being, the body. This also led to the discussion of when a person was actually dead and whether they could still be anointed after their last breath. The thinking was that the

---

57. Martos, 336.
58. See Martos, 338.
59. Gusmer, 29.
60. See Martos, 338.

soul lingered in this life for a brief time and that one could be anointed within an hour, more or less, after their final breath. This practice continued until the revised rite of 1972 was implemented.

It was generally understood that Jesus had instituted this sacrament, but Aquinas reasoned that since there was no mention of Jesus doing so in the Gospel accounts then he must have left it to James and the other Apostles to make it known to the Church.[61] This became a point of disagreement between the reformers of the sixteenth century and the bishops of the Council of Trent.

The Council of Trent

The Council of Trent (1545–1563) did very little to change either the practice or the theological understandings associated with the Anointing of the Sick. The Council accepted the common designation of the sacrament as Extreme Unction, often called the Last Rites, and its intent to prepare persons for death.

Concerning the issue of its institution, the Council maintained that it was instituted by Christ and announced by the Apostle James. Both Martin Luther and John Calvin disputed this claim saying that James was speaking of an anointing of the "sick" and not of the "dying," and unless it had a specific direction from Jesus it could not be called a sacrament. Luther and Calvin did allow that it could be considered a sacramental of the Church. Such as the use of holy water, anointing, therefore, could have some spiritual benefit, such as a feeling of consolation for the sick person. They also believed that anointing could effect the forgiveness of sins, but only because of the person's confidence in God and faith in divine mercy, not from the power of the rite.[62] Some Lutheran congregations today celebrate a rite of anointing, both at Baptism and when a person is sick.

> Now, this sacred unction of the sick was instituted by Christ our Lord, as truly and properly a sacrament of the new law, insinuated indeed in Mark, but recommended and promulgated to the faithful by James the Apostle, and brother of the Lord.
>
> —Council of Trent

---

61. See Martos, 337.
62. See Martos, 339.

The position of the Council of Trent was stated in four canons:

- Extreme unction is a sacrament instituted by Christ and announced by James.
- The sacrament has an enduring salvific meaning in terms of conferring grace, remitting sins, and comforting the sick.
- The rite and practice of the sacrament correspond with the scriptural precedent in James.
- The proper minister of the anointing is the priest.[63]

It is interesting to note that the Council's official position on the sacrament does not mention that its application is only for those who are in danger of death. An additional canon sates: "this anointing is to be administered to the sick, especially to those who are so dangerously ill that they seem near to death."[64]

During the centuries that followed the Council of Trent, there was no change in the doctrine of Extreme Unction, and, despite the allowance that it could be administered to those who were sick, there was no change in the practice of anointing as preparation for death. The appearance of the priest at the bedside of the sick person was an indication that in fact death was imminent; and often seen as a way to convey bad news to the sick person without really telling them.

Two other issues taken up by theologians in the centuries following the Council of Trent were the age when a person could be anointed and whether a person could be anointed when their death seemed apparent but not definitive.

On the question of the appropriate age, an allowance was made that those who had reached the age of discretion could be anointed. Prior to this time, it was believed that children were not capable of committing sin, hence there was no need to be anointed. In practice, this meant that they

> This unction is to be applied to the sick, but to those especially who lie in such danger as to seem to be about to depart this life: whence also it is called the sacrament of the departing. And if the sick should, after having received this unction, recover, they may again be aided by the succour of this sacrament, when they fall into another like danger of death.
>
> —Council of Trent

---

63. See Gusmer, 33.
64. Gusmer, 34.

could be anointed after they had made their first confession, which was celebrated at any time from the age of seven to sixteen.[65] This pastoral practice
clearly reflected the understanding that the Anointing of the Sick was primarily for the forgiveness of sin and not for healing.

On the question of when to anoint, there were two opinions. One opinion was that a person should show some signs of life in order for the sacrament to have any spiritual effect. A second opinion reflected the earlier
thinking, namely that the soul could linger in the body for some time, even
after vital functions had ceased. A safer course was widely adapted since there
was no certain way of determining the exact moment of death and priests
were encouraged to conditionally anoint those who seemed to be dead but
maybe were not fully deceased.[66] In such circumstances, priests often believed
that anointing a person who was obviously dead brought more comfort and
peace to the living. This position meant that at some point it was necessary
to place oneself in the mercy of God who would surely take care of anyone
once they had died.

The key shift in the pastoral practice and liturgical theology of the
medieval era, one that was reaffirmed by Trent, is best summed up in the
words of Joseph Martos: "The anointing of the sick, which had begun in the
patristic era as a door to the sacred meaning of sickness, became, in the modern church, a door to the sacred meaning of dying."[67]

The Reformed Rite of the Second Vatican Council

The stirrings of change that eventually led to the widespread reform of the
liturgy, began in the latter half of the nineteenth century. Although the initial focus was on how to enable a fuller participation by the lay faithful in the
liturgy, this liturgical renewal eventually became more encompassing. An
aggiornamento,[68] or bringing up-to-date, was in turn supported by the advocacy of scholars in Scripture, Church history and, of course, the liturgy.

Biblical scholars observed that the meaning of death found in the
New Testament was less "doleful than the medieval interpretation of it."[69]
Liturgical scholars pointed out that there seemed to be a discrepancy between

---

65. See Martos, 341.

66. See Martos, 339–340.

67. Martos, 342.

68. *Aggiornamento* (an Italian word) came to refer to "throwing open the windows of the Church,"
a phrase that was used by Pope John XXIII in January 1959 when he announced his desire for a Council.

69. Martos, 343.

the meanings and the accounts of healing in the biblical texts, especially those in Jesus' ministry, and the subsequent emphasis on dying that had informed the Church's rite since the Middle Ages. Historians challenged the notion that the Rite of Anointing had always been intended as a preparation for death, saying that the historical evidence of the early Church indicated a different practice than that in later centuries, one that the Council of Trent had left in place.

By the middle of the twentieth century these various threads of thought had found their way into publications and discussions and soon a new energy evolved known as *resourcement* ("a return to earlier sources"). A number of questions arose surrounding the theology and the practice of Extreme Unction: Should it be a sacrament for the sick, as in the early Church, as well as or instead of only for those preparing to die? Should anointing be the last sacrament before death instead of Viaticum? Should the Patristic era be revisited and a new emphasis be given to the healing power of anointing within life and not just at the end of life? Had the Rite of Anointing become more individualized and less communal in its pastoral practice? And, was the name of the sacrament, Extreme Unction, the best one to convey new understandings and practices related to the Church's care of the sick and the dying?

The reform of the sacrament of Extreme Unction was included in the broader revision of all the sacramental rites of the Church. In three short paragraphs[70] the Council directed that specific changes be applied to Extreme Unction, thereby reforming both its theology and practice.

"Extreme Unction" which may also and more properly be called "Anointing of the Sick," is not a sacrament for those only who are at the point of death. Hence, as soon as any one of the faithful begins to be in danger of death from sickness or old age, the fitting time for that person to receive this sacrament has certainly already arrived.[71]

In addition to the separate rites for Anointing of the Sick and for Viaticum, a continuous rite shall be drawn up, structured so that the sick person is anointed after confessing and before receiving Viaticum.[72]

---

70. See the *Constitution on the Sacred Liturgy* (CSL), 73–75.
71. CSL, 73.
72. CSL, 74.

The number of the anointings is to be adapted to the circumstances; the prayers that belong to the rite of anointing are to be so revised that they correspond to the varying conditions of the sick who receive the sacrament.[73]

In November 1972, Pope Paul VI established a new sacramental form for the Anointing of the Sick. In the course of the next ten years the member conferences of the International Commission on English in the Liturgy (ICEL) proposed additional changes. These additions included newly composed prayers intended to make the rite more pastorally effective within various pastoral circumstances. An English translation of the revision of the *editio typica* (typical edition) of 1972 was approved by the National Conference of Catholic Bishops (US) in November 1982, and confirmed by the Sacred Congregation for the Sacraments and Divine Worship in December of the same year. It is this rite, known as *Pastoral Care of the Sick: Rites of Anointing and Viaticum* that is currently in use in the English speaking dioceses of the United States.

The new rite, which is outlined and explored in the next section, grew out of the three Conciliar statements referenced above. Here is a summary of the revisions adopted by the Council:

- The name for the sacrament was changed from Extreme Unction to Anointing of the Sick.

- Additional rites were added: for example, visits to the sick; visits to a sick child; Communion to the sick[74]; celebration of Viaticum and rites for exceptional circumstances.

- In response to the shift in theological emphasis from preparation for death to attending to the sick, many new prayers were composed to suit various pastoral circumstances.

- The overall pastoral focus was placed within the broader context of the healing ministry of the Church.

- Communal anointing celebrations are encouraged as they underline the ecclesial nature of the sacrament.

- With the emphasis on the sacrament being for those who are sick, and not those near death, the sacrament was to be celebrated sooner than later.

---

73. CSL, 75.

74. For a thorough treatment of the history of Communion to the Sick, refer to *Guide for Celebrating Worship of the Eucharist outside Mass* by John Thomas Lane, sss, published by Liturgy Training Publications.

The Rite of Anointing is to be celebrated in a communal setting, even if it does not take place at Mass.

- There was no specific liturgical site designated for anointing. The various rites could be celebrated in any place, depending on the pastoral circumstances and the state of health of the person(s) to be anointed.

- Even if the rite is not celebrated in a communal setting, for example, within Mass, others who are ministering to the sick person, such as family members or caregivers are encouraged to be present and to pray over the one who is sick.

- Viaticum is once again regarded as the sacrament of the dying and, in most circumstances, is to be given as the last sacrament.

- In keeping with the overall reform of the sacramental rites, various options are included in the rite for a wide range of pastoral situations.[75]

- The Anointing of the Sick can be repeated, since it is a sacrament of strengthening and healing of the whole person.

- The gesture for anointing and the places where a person is anointed is specified.

- The oil for anointing is to be blessed by the bishop. However, a priest may bless the oil for anointing during the actual rite.

---

75. See CSL, 38.

- The ordinary minister of the sacrament is the priest; there is no extraordinary minister.

- The ordinary minister of Viaticum is the priest; however, allowance is made for an extraordinary minister, such as a deacon or lay person.

Theological Principles in the Rite of Anointing

Having outlined some of the developments that led to a renewal of the Sacrament of the Anointing of the Sick, and noting the extensive revisions of the rite, it seems appropriate to explore the liturgical theology within the rite before describing the various elements in its celebration.

Perhaps the most important change in the Sacrament of the Anointing of the Sick was situating it within the broader pastoral context of the ministry of the Church. This ministry not only includes the Anointing of the Sick but other expressions of pastoral care by all members of the Church for those who are sick. In these several ways the whole Church continues the ministry of Jesus himself.

Flowing from this ecclesiology is the encouragement to celebrate the sacrament in a communal setting. The *Constitution on the Sacred Liturgy* stated that the communal celebration of the liturgy, especially the Mass and the sacraments, was preferred over a celebration that is individual and private.[76] Prior to the revisions of the Second Vatican Council the practice of anointing a sick person was almost always a private action, including only the priest and the sick person. The newly revised ritual seeks to make the prayerful participation by other people more expressive of the concern of the Church for the sick person and a more visible sign to the sick person of comfort, support, and compassion. Martos calls this character of the sacrament a more experiential than a doctrinal aspect.[77] Those who participate in the sacrament, either by being anointed or by engaging in the ritual prayers, are affected by the existential nature of the celebration. They are conscious of the working of the

Those who are seriously ill need the special help of God's grace in this time of anxiety, lest they be broken in spirit and, under the pressure of temptation, perhaps weakened in their faith.

—*Pastoral Care of the Sick*, 5

76. See CSL, 26.
77. Martos, 347.

The collective prayer of the Church assures the sick that they are loved and that God cares for them.

Holy Spirit within the human condition and are thus recipients of the grace of the Risen Lord.

The collective prayer of the Church not only assures the person who is sick that they are loved, but also expresses the concern of God for those who suffer in body and spirit. The spiritual nature of the sacrament is rooted in the suffering of Christ, and a reminder that we are all participants in the Paschal Mystery. This also means that pain, suffering, and even death are not the last word for the faithful disciple of the Lord. The sacrament calls forth a renewal of that faith in God who sent his son to gather us into his loving embrace as a shepherd gathers a lamb in his arms. Many priests and pastoral care ministers can recall comments from those who have been anointed of how they experienced a feeling of peace and surrender after having been anointed. They have attributed this to a sense that it was Christ himself who was present in the words and actions of the rite. And so he was!

One of the theological questions that is not directly answered by the reformed rite is whether it effects physical healing or spiritual healing or both. The prayers and readings for the Rite of Anointing, as we shall see in a later treatment, speak of regaining strength, of being raised up, of being restored to health, and of the person returning to former duties. If these outcomes are to happen, and in many situations they do, then there is a certain physical restoration that follows the rite of anointing. But does the sacrament bring about such a physical change, or is it part of the body's own ability to recover from sickness coupled with medical intervention? It has been noted that the experience of those who have been anointed has almost always been a more spiritual awareness of being better, even if a physical recovery is not immediate or even foreseeable. It is helpful to remember a couple of things here. First, there is a difference between being cured of an illness and being healed. The former indicates that the cause of the illness is eradicated, never to return. Yet the rite suggests that anointing can recur as often as the person feels ill, seeming to indicate that a cure is not what is intended by the sacrament. The pastoral notes of the rite offer this comment: A return to physical health *may* follow the reception of this sacrament if it will be beneficial to the sick person's salvation.[78] A different notion of healing seems to be intended by the rite. Such a healing effect is possible whether or not the person is cured. This healing is more of a spiritual nature, allowing the sick person to be free of anxiety, of fear for the future, or of being alone or discouraged.

> Through the Sacrament of Anointing, Christ strengthens the faithful who are afflicted by illness, providing them with the strongest means of support.
>
> —*Pastoral Care of the Sick*, 5

For all of us, being sick is a surrender both to the Lord and to the care of others. It is a sign of human vulnerability, and it challenges us to a level of trust that is recognized in the prayers and actions of the rite. We know from Christ's own words that human sickness has meaning and value for our salvation and through it we come to participate in his resurrection to eternal life. The rite puts those who are anointed, and those who surround them, in touch with the love of Christ who so often and so generously extended compassion to those who came to him to be healed of their infirmities.

Moreover, the sacrament is based on Christian hope, not on human desire, as well intentioned as that may be. The person who is sick and who seeks to be anointed, and those who care for them, are people of faith. The request to be anointed is an act of faith. It is a declaration of trust in the will of God, of believing that God truly cares for our well-being, and of accepting that we will be given the grace to endure sickness with God's help.

---

78.   See PCS, 6.

Although there is a close relationship between the Sacraments of Penance and Anointing, the two are not interchangeable.

One issue that remains an ongoing theological discussion is the relationship between the Anointing of the Sick and the forgiveness of sins. The Sacrament of Penance and the Sacrament of the Anointing the Sick are closely related. In practice a person may confess their sins prior to being anointed, or as part of the celebration of anointing. However, in some circumstances, if the person being anointed is not able to confess sin, then those sins are forgiven through the Sacrament of Anointing. Both Penance and Anointing are sacraments of healing; though the Church doesn't regard them as interchangeable. However, the forgiveness of sin through the Rite of Anointing is envisioned in the rite.

Preparing the Rites of the Sick

"The Lord himself showed great concern for the for the bodily and spiritual
welfare of the sick and commanded his followers to do likewise."

—*Pastoral Care of the Sick: Rites of Anointing and Viaticum*, 5

The ritual book that is needed for pastoral ministers to care for the sick
is *Pastoral Care of the Sick: Rites of Anointing and Viaticum*. The title
gives a clear indication that this ritual is more than a simple Rite of
Anointing. The term "pastoral care" certainly includes more than a single
rite and involves a broader ministry within the parish than that of the priest.
The opening words of the decree promulgating the reformed rite indicate
that pastoral care of the sick belongs to the ministry of the whole Church:
"When the Church cares for the sick, it serves Christ himself in the suffering
members of His Mystical Body."[1] The role of the pastoral care minister,
whether a priest, deacon, or lay person, is an important ministry in the
life of the Church. The pastoral care minister represents the presence and
support of the faith community and is a visible sign of the compassion of
Christ himself.

The pastoral care minister is also the presider for the various rites associated with the care of the sick: the Sacraments of Anointing and Viaticum,
Communion, Reconciliation, blessings, and so on. As the leader of prayer,
whether in a communal setting or in an individual instance with a sick or
dying person, he or she extends an invitation to prayer and enters the ritual
dialogue that constitutes a liturgical act of the Church.

The pastoral care minister performs a pastoral role; that is, he or she is
not a parent or a "fixer" of the illness. They do not talk down to the sick person or make empty promises that "all will be well." The minister portrays the
image of the Good Shepherd, being compassionate and encouraging without
downplaying the human reality of illness and the toll it takes on the emotions and spiritual health of the person.

---

1. Sacred Congregation for Divine Worship, decree *Pastoral Care of the Sick, Rites of Anointing
and Viaticum*, paragraph 3.

The minister knows the rite and uses it gracefully, always being sensitive to the circumstances surrounding each celebration, and making adaptations that are most suitable for the sick person.

The minster recognizes that praying with the sick and the dying is a privileged moment, and that the sick and the dying, and those who accompany them are often fragile in the face of suffering and the possibility of death.

It goes without saying that the minister does not wear a mask of indifference. He or she must have a strong spiritual sense of their own comfort level with the presence of suffering in the world, and be able to speak sincerely about their faith in the merciful goodness of God. The minister's own spirituality is based on reverence for each person as a child of God, and for the moment as a time of holiness. This is a posture of humility; he or she is a vehicle of the mercy of Christ. This can be called the attitude of transparency, the recognition that it is Christ who heals, forgives, and restores the person to wholeness. At the same time the minister acknowledges that there is weakness in all of humanity, but the gift of grace and the action of the Holy Spirit is greater than human brokenness and that there is nothing beyond the redemptive love of God. He or she assures the sick and the dying that God's plan of salvation means that God has not forgotten them, that their illness is not punishment for any sin, and that they need not be afraid. Finally, the pastoral care minister is a person of prayer. The minister's own spiritual health is very important; she or he must cultivate a familiarity with God if they are to bring the healing presence of God to others through the sacraments of the Church.

> It is thus fitting that all baptized Christians share in this ministry of mutual charity within the Body of Christ by doing all that they can to help the sick return to health, by showing love for the sick, and by celebrating the sacraments with them.
>
> —*Pastoral Care of the Sick*, 33

The Preparation Team

The pastoral care minister is part of a parish or hospital team. Although *Pastoral Care of the Sick* certainly allows for anointing to take place when only the priest and the person who is sick are involved, it envisions other times when there are communal celebrations of the sacrament. Even in the case of an individual anointing, it is likely that one or more persons, such as

Communal celebrations should involve liturgical ministers.

health care attendants or family members, are present. Communal celebrations involve those liturgical ministers who normally assist with the necessary preparations for other parish liturgies, including members of the worship team, environment team, musicians, readers, greeters, and presiders. Some parishes have the resources to employ a pastoral care coordinator. This person takes the initiative for scheduling and preparing celebrations of the Anointing of the Sick. He or she works closely with the liturgy coordinator, who in turn involves the parish music ministry and liturgical ministers (greeters, readers, and extraordinary ministers of Holy Communion). If there are volunteer pastoral care visitors then one or more of them may assist with the celebration, especially if it takes place outside the church, for example in a chapel or in an appropriate gathering space in a nursing home or health care residence. Another member of the team may be the deacon. If there is a parish nurse then she or he should definitely be involved with the preparation and celebration of anointing.

Pastoral care is a broadly based ministry in the Church, so it is reasonable to expect that many people need to be involved with the actual efforts that provide such care. Christian ministry, in all its expressions, is the embodiment of the hands and feet of Christ in the midst of the people of God. The task of the parish team is to gather the people and their respective ministries so that those who are sick will benefit from the healing and prayerful love of the Body of Christ.

Resources for the Parish Team

The pastoral care team should familiarize themselves with the ritual book, *Pastoral Care of the Sick: Rites of Anointing and Viaticum.* It is s comprised of three parts and an appendix:

- Part 1: Pastoral Care of the Sick
- Part 2: Pastoral Care of the Dying
- Part 3: Readings, Responses, and Verses from Sacred Scripture
- Appendix: Rite of Reconciliation of Individual Penitents

The first two parts are further divided into chapters. Part 1, Pastoral Care of the Sick, includes Visits to the Sick (chapter 1), Visits to a Sick Child (chapter 2), Communion of the Sick (chapter 3), and Anointing of the Sick (chapter 4). There are two rites for bringing Communion to the sick: one for ordinary circumstances, for example, if the sick person is homebound, and the other for when the person is in a hospital or an institution. Chapter 4 includes three rites for anointing: one for anointing outside Mass; one for anointing within Mass; and one for anointing in a hospital or institution. Part 2, Pastoral Care of the Dying, includes the Celebration of Viaticum (chapter 5), the Commendation of the Dying (chapter 6), Prayers for the Dead (chapter 7), and the Rites for Exceptional Circumstances (chapter 8).

In addition to *Pastoral Care of the Sick*, pastoral care teams will need to be familiar with several other ritual books in order to explore the many options that the Church provides for the sick and opportunities for prayer such as the Mass formularies in *The Roman Missal*, the readings in the *Lectionary for Mass*, and the rites in the *Order of Christian Funerals, Rite of Penance, Order of Confirmation, Rite of Baptism for Children, Rite of Christian Initiation of Adults,* and the various blessings in the *Book of Blessings.* Ministers should also be familiar with liturgical documents such as the *Constitution on the Sacred Liturgy, General Instruction of the Roman Missal, Built of Living Stones,* and *Sing to the Lord: Music in Divine Worship.*

Celebrating the Rites

Overview of the Ritual Text

Pastoral Care of the Sick offers the Church a rich treasury of ritual assistance for visiting the sick, praying with them, bringing them Communion or

Viaticum, and offering them the opportunity for Reconciliation and being anointed. It has a strong pastoral character that is evident in the celebrations of the various rites. Each rite is placed within the context of pastoral circumstances giving the ministers a range of choices for the prayers, readings, and even the length of the respective rite.

A second characteristic of the various rites is that they are intended to be communal celebrations. Individual celebrations are certainly allowed, and in practice often happen, but are seen as the exception. The rites for the sick are liturgical acts of the Church. This is underscored by the inclusion of readings from Scripture; the role of a presider, whether a priest, deacon, or lay pastoral minister; the place for music, when appropriate; the emphasis on the prayer of faith by those who are present; the liturgical gestures of blessing and the laying on of hands; the prayers that invite a response from participants; and the use of the sacramental symbol of blessed oil.

> Like the other sacraments, these too have a community aspect, which should be brought out as much as possible when they are celebrated.
>
> —*Pastoral Care of the Sick*, 33

With respect to the role of the leader of the different rites, the rubrics use three words: priest, deacon, and minister. The priest is the ordinary and only minister of the Sacrament of Anointing and of Penance. When Anointing and Penance are not celebrated, a deacon or a lay person may preside in the absence of a priest. In those situations when the rite does not call for an ordained person then the word minister is used. This may refer to the leader of the celebration, the person who reads from Scripture, a lay pastoral visitor, the person who offers a reflection on the Scripture reading, or the person who assists in other ways with the rite.

There are no restrictions for when pastoral visits of the sick, including Communion of the sick, can take place. Likewise, Anointing of the Sick may be celebrated whenever there is a need to do so. However, communal celebrations of anointing outside Mass are not allowed during the Sacred Triduum. At other times, pastoral reasons should dictate when it is appropriate for communal celebrations outside Mass to take place. For example, Christmas, Ash Wednesday, Easter Sunday, or any other Sunday may not be the most suitable days for a communal Anointing of the Sick. The ritual Mass for the Anointing of the Sick is not permitted during the days of Holy Week, on the solemnities of Christmas, Epiphany, Ascension, Pentecost, the Most Holy Body and Blood of Christ, Holydays of Obligation, Ash Wednesday, and the Sundays of Advent, Lent, and Easter Time.

The place for the rites of pastoral care, including the Anointing of the Sick, is not specified in the rubrics. The assumption is that ordinarily the rites take place wherever the sick person is present. The abilities of those who are sick will determine whether they can gather in a chapel or common room in a health care institution or even at the parish church.

The liturgical environment for the celebration of the rites of the sick

The liturgical year should guide the celebration of the rites held in the parish church.

is usually relatively simple. If it is a communal celebration in the church, then some attention should be given to the setting keeping in mind the principles governing the liturgical season or day in the liturgical year.

The inclusion of liturgical music is always appropriate whenever the Church gathers to pray. The celebration of the rites for the sick is certainly a good time for music that accompanies the prayers and adds to the spiritual character of the occasion. If it is well chosen and presented in a suitable manner, music can have a healing and calming effect on the person who is sick and on those who are participating in the rite. Certainly there should be music for those communal celebrations, whether within or outside Mass. A number of psalms and antiphons are provided in part three of the rite; although, there is no listing of hymns. The music ministry of each parish will have resources from which to select music that relates to the liturgical season as well as the hope, healing, and the compassion of the Lord for those who suffer and are ill.[2]

---

2. See *Sing to the Lord: Music in Divine Worship*, 227–228.

Part 1: Pastoral Care of the Sick

"The rites in Part I of *Pastoral Care of the sick: Rites of Anointing and Viaticum* are used by the Church to comfort the sick in time of anxiety, to encourage them to fight against illness, and perhaps to restore them to health."[3] The rites in Part 1 express the concern that "Christ showed for the bodily and spiritual welfare of those who were ill,"[4] a compassion that is continued by the Church in her ministry to the sick. Concern for those who suffer and are sick is a social issue for the human family and one that is of particular interest for the family of faith when one of her members is ill. But, concern for the sick is more than thoughtful attentiveness—it is a ministry of all Christians "who should visit the sick, remember them in prayer, and celebrate the sacraments with them."[5] This ministry includes many people: the family and friends of the one who is sick, health care professionals who care for the sick, and those who have pastoral responsibilities for the spiritual well-being of members of the Church.

Chapter 1: Visits to the Sick

Outline of the Rite

- Reading
- Response
- The Lord's Prayer
- Concluding Prayer
- Blessing

The Rite for Visits to the Sick is relatively brief. However, it is more than a friendly drop-in by the pastoral visitor, whether a lay minister, priest, or deacon. The request for a visit often comes from the sick person themselves or from a family member. The presence of the pastoral visitor indicates that the larger faith community cares about all her members and desires to reach out to those who are not able to be present in the Eucharistic assembly. In order to include the sick person in the life of the Church, the minister may ask them to pray for others who are suffering, for the leaders of the Church, and for those who are praying for them. In this way, the sick person is able to offer

---

3. PCS, 42.
4. PCS, 43.
5. PCS, 43.

their time of suffering as a way to be united with Christ and with their brothers and sisters in faith.

The rite does not envision that Communion, Reconciliation, or Anointing are included in this visit. If Communion, Reconciliation, or Anointing is to take place then it is wise for the pastoral visitor to have that information ahead of time. Sometimes a sick person assumes that a pastoral visitor will bring Communion for them and will be upset if that does not take place. If the parish has a pastoral care coordinator then he or she should communicate with both the sick person and the pastoral visitor, and prepare for those rites to be celebrated (and for an ordained minister to visit the sick person, if necessary).

A lay minister may lead the rite and he or she may be accompanied by one or more parish visitors. The leader is usually a person who is familiar with the person who is sick and who has established a congenial rapport with them.

The rite itself does not include an opening greeting or exchange between the visitor and the person who is sick. It is assumed that some form of initial greeting does indeed take place, making sure that it is hospitable, avoiding any semblance of being hurried or perfunctory. Even if the visitor is visiting more than one person, for example in a nursing home, each person should be greeted before the rite is celebrated.

The rite begins with a reading from Scripture, either one of the options provided in the rite itself or from those provided in the appendix. The rubrics note that either the minister or someone else who is present may read the Scripture text. A brief period of silence may be observed after the reading, followed by one of the psalms provided in the rite or from the appendix. The minister may then give a short explanation of the reading, being aware of the ability of the sick person to be attentive. The minister then leads those who are present, including the sick person, if they are able, with the praying of the Lord's Prayer. The Lord's Prayer concludes with one of three options for a closing prayer and then the minister leads the final blessing. If the minister is a priest or deacon he may lay hands on the head of the sick person and make the Sign of the Cross over them. If the minister is not a priest or deacon he or she makes the Sign of the Cross on himself or herself and traces the

> The ministers should encourage the sick person to offer his or her sufferings in union with Christ and to join in prayer for the Church and the world.
>
> —*Pastoral Care of the Sick*, 56

Sign of the Cross on the forehead of the sick person. Although not mentioned in the rite, unless the person is too ill, it is appropriate to sing a familiar hymn at the beginning and end of this prayer service.

Chapter 2: Visits to a Sick Child

Outline of the Rite

- Reading
- Response
- The Lord's Prayer
- Concluding Prayer
- Blessing

The Rite for Visits to a Sick Child follows the same format as the one for Visits to the Sick. The rite allows for a range of adaptations, depending on the circumstances of the child's illness, their ability to understand their situation, and their readiness to participate in the rite itself. It is good pastoral practice for the visitor to spend a few moments in informal conversation with the child before the rite is celebrated. If the child is sick enough that a pastoral visit is appropriate, it might be assumed that the parents or guardians are concerned for the welfare of their child. This may require that the pastoral visitor spend some time with the parents and any other family members in order to offer them the comfort and assurance of God's love and of the prayerful support of their Church family. Parental permission should be secured before visiting with the child and the minister should have participated in parish or diocesan level VIRTUS or other forms of protecting God's children training programs.

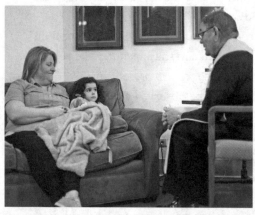

The pastoral minister may spend time with the parents to offer support.

The Scripture readings provided in the rite speak of Jesus' concern for children and his observation that all persons are children before God. The rite provides other options as well.[6] Following the reading, a short period of silence may be observed and the minister might offer an explanation of the reading. If the child is old enough to understand their illness they could be invited to be part of the discussion, even offering their opinion on the Scripture reading. The responsory that follows is a short litany with invocations and a response. In order for those present, including the child, to participate, the minister will need to bring a worship aid or a copy of the ritual text. The minister then leads the Lord's Prayer, a concluding prayer, and offers the final blessing. There are two options for the concluding prayer; the words express the loving concern of God for all of us and especially for the child who is sick.

In the first option for the final blessing, the minister makes the Sign of the Cross on the child's forehead, refers to him or her by name, and says: "when you were baptized, / you were marked with the cross of Jesus. / I make this cross / on your forehead / and ask the Lord to bless you, / and restore you to health."[7] The rubrics note that those who are present may also make the Sign of the Cross on the child's forehead in silence. If the minister is a priest or deacon he imparts a blessing by laying hands on the child. A lay minister invokes God's blessing and makes the Sign of the Cross on himself or herself.[8]

The experience of a sick child can be very traumatic for a family; but the resilience of children and their likelihood of recovery are also realities. Often children are able to accept their situation and are capable of uplifting the spirits of others. If the circumstances allow, and parents agree, then other family members could be present for the pastoral

> The minister should help sick children understand that the sick are very special in the eyes of God because they are suffering as Christ suffered and because they can offer their sufferings for the salvation of the world.
>
> —*Pastoral Care of the Sick*, 64

visit—siblings, a close childhood friend, and grandparents can help the sick child feel included in the life of their family even in illness.

The pastoral visit to a person who is sick, no matter their age, reminds all of us that we are instruments of the mercy of God. Moreover, it is a sign

---

6. See PCS, 66.
7. PCS, 70A.
8. See PCS, 61.

that we have taken to heart the teaching of Jesus who told us, "When I was sick, you visited me."[9]

Chapter 3: Communion of the Sick

The practice of giving Communion to those who are sick is rooted in the Church's ministerial obligation to care for those who are unable to participate in the community's celebration of the Eucharist. This is precisely the reason why additional hosts are consecrated at Mass and reserved in the tabernacle for the sick. Participation in the parish Eucharistic celebration is "their rightful and accustomed place."[10] The role of the pastoral minister in visiting the sick imitates the ministry of Jesus. In bringing Holy Communion to the sick "the minister of communion represents Christ and manifests faith and charity on behalf of the whole community" and extends to the sick person "a sign of support and concern" from the whole community for one of her members.[11]

Pastoral Care of the Sick provides two rites for bringing Communion to the sick when they cannot attend Sunday Mass; one in ordinary circumstances and one for use in hospitals or institutions. Although the pastoral notes in the rite suggest that Mass be celebrated in the home of the sick person with their families and friends,[12] the rites that are provided take place within the context of a Liturgy of the Word. In practice, celebrating Mass in the home is often the exception. Since *Pastoral Care of the Sick* was first introduced into the life of the Church, there have been great strides in the field of health care and there is a growing trend for those who are sick to receive support from families and health care agencies while remaining in their own home. This situation, coupled with the

The role of the pastoral minister is to imitate Jesus.

---

9. See Matthew 25:36 (author's paraphrase).
10. PCS, 73.
11. PCS, 73.
12. See PCS, 77.

growing shortage of priests, means that the possibility of home Masses is less likely than before. At the same time, there has been a wonderful increase in the number of people involved in pastoral care ministries within their respective communities and parishes. This has made it possible for those confined to their homes because of illness to receive the prayerful support and concern of the Church.

When bringing Communion to the sick, the minister must transport the consecrated host in a pyx (a small metal vessel) or another closed container. The rubrics specifically state that the Blessed Sacrament is to be placed on a table covered with a "linen cloth."[13] Presumably, a member of the family of the sick person, a health care assistant, or the sick person is aware of the pastoral minister's visit and can prepare the setting. Although the rite recommends lighted candles to be placed near the Blessed Sacrament, this may not always be possible, especially in a hospital or institution. Pastoral ministers will need to secure permission from health care professionals. The rite also suggests a vessel of holy water could be placed on the table (if this is used in the Introductory Rite). Ministers could also add an icon of Jesus, Mary, the saints, or a crucifix. "Care should be taken to make the occasion special and joyful."[14] It's best if the table is near the sick person's bed or chair.

> The links between the community's Eucharistic celebration, especially on the Lord's Day, and the communion of the sick are intimate and manifold.
>
> —*Pastoral Care of the Sick*, 73

There may be situations in which the person (or persons) are unable to receive the consecrated host and are only able to receive the Precious Blood. Pastoral Care of the Sick does allow for these situations. It should be carried in a vessel that is "properly covered" so that there is no danger of it being spilled and remaining Precious Blood should be consumed immediately after the rite. The pastoral care minister should also make sure that the vessel is properly purified by the parish priest or deacon.[15]

---

13. PCS, 74.
14. PCS, 74.
15. See PCS, 74.

Outline of the Rite

Introductory Rites

- Greeting
- Sprinkling with Holy Water
- Penitential Rite

Liturgy of the Word

- Reading
- Response
- General Intercessions

Liturgy of Holy Communion

- The Lord's Prayer
- Communion
- Silent Prayer
- Prayer after Communion

Concluding Rite

- Blessing

The first option provided in chapter 3 is Communion in Ordinary Circumstances. This rite is relatively simple. A selection of prayers and readings are provided for the celebration. The minister may choose from the ones in the specific rite or from those in the appendix. As part of the preparation for the celebration, the sick person or others may select the prayers and readings. The rubrics do not specify who the "others" might be; however, a spouse or another family member are the obvious ones to assist in preparing for the celebration. The reading may be proclaimed by the minister or by someone else who is present. However, for the intercessions, the rubrics give preference to someone other than the minister.[16]

The sprinkling with holy water is optional, although its use clearly recalls the Sacrament of Baptism and reminds all present that we are baptized into the passion, death, and Resurrection of Christ.

If a priest is present for this rite then he may inquire if the sick person wishes to celebrate the Sacrament of Reconciliation. If so, the sacrament takes

---

16. See PCS, 86.

place instead of the Penitential Act. The pastoral minister should inquire about the sick person's wishes prior to this visit so that he or she will not be disappointed if a priest does not arrive. Two options are provided for the Penitential Act. Ministers should be aware that since *Pastoral Care of the Sick* has yet to be retranslated, the translation of the Confiteor provided in the rite should be updated with that from the third edition of *The Roman Missal*. There are worship aids avail-

The minister may give a short homily or explanation of the reading.

able that pastoral care ministers can use when they celebrate Communion of the Sick. These worship aids can be purchased in large quantities and may be given to those who gather for this celebration.

The rite notes that one reading is proclaimed. The options that are provided are Eucharistic in theme. The minister may give a brief reflection or explanation of the reading, drawing a connection between Christ as the bread of life and his Eucharistic presence in the lives of believers. The Eucharist is the sacramental sign of God's promise to be our strength at all times, especially in our suffering and sickness. In order to connect the ill person with the Sunday assembly, ministers may also consider proclaiming the Gospel from the past Sunday.

The intercessions themselves are not provided in the rite. The petitions will need to be prepared ahead of time or the pastoral minister may offer spontaneous petitions and invite those present to add their own intentions. The pastoral notes in the rite include a reminder that the state of the sick person is to be considered when choosing the reading as well as determining the length of the explanation of the reading. The focus of the entire celebration is to bring comfort and solace to the person who is sick; the rite allows for adaptations with that in mind.

The liturgy of Holy Communion begins with the Lord's Prayer and all those who are gathered should be invited to pray it together. The Lord's Prayer is so familiar to Catholics, and indeed all Christians, that pastoral ministers will attest to the fact that even when a sick person is frail and unable to participate fully in the other parts of the rite, they will respond with a new found energy in praying this prayer.

After the Lord's Prayer, the pastoral minister presents the consecrated bread to the person by using one of two formulas. The second option is the same one that is used during the Communion Rite at Mass, although the text in the rite is the former translation. The minister should know the words of the new translation from the Missal and use them at this time.

In most circumstances, the sick person will be able to receive the consecrated host, but in those situations in which they might experience difficulty swallowing there are other options. Communion bread producers provide various sizes of hosts and a smaller one could be used (priests will need to know ahead of time so that they can be consecrated at Sunday Mass). Another option is to offer the sick person a portion of the host and place it on his or her tongue so that it may dissolve easily in their mouth. The person may be offered water to help consume the host. Another option is for the sick person to receive the Precious Blood instead of the host. If this is the case, then the minister needs to have a worthy and secure container in which to transport the Precious Blood from the church. Since the Precious Blood is not normally reserved in the tabernacle following Mass, arrangements need to be made so that there is a convenient way for the minister to access a small amount for Communion of the sick.

Other persons who are participating in the celebration may also receive Communion at this time. The minister should inquire ahead of time as to how many will be receiving Communion in order to bring enough hosts. Any remaining hosts or Precious Blood should be consumed. The rubrics call for a period of silence after Communion. Allowing for moments of silence during the celebration, both at this point and after the reading, indicate that the celebration need not appear hurried. This is also a sign of respect for the sick person and a gesture of sensitivity that says that their world, where illness slows one down, is just as important as that of those who are well.

After the period of silence, the minister offers the Prayer after Communion and the concluding rite takes place. The rite provides two options for the final blessing when celebrated by a priest or deacon. These options include four intercessions. If there is still one or more consecrated hosts in the pyx (because the minister has one or more additional visits) then a blessing may be given using the pyx. The blessing with the pyx is done in silence. If the minister is not a priest or deacon then different words are used for the final blessing, and the minister makes the Sign of the Cross on himself or herself.

Communion in a Hospital or Institution

The pastoral notes envision that this rite is celebrated when there are a number of communicants in the same residence, hospital, or other health care institution.[17] The ideal situation allows for all those who are to receive Communion to gather in one place such as a chapel or other suitable space. In this way, the rite is celebrated once and Communion is given to each communicant. If those present are not able to gather in one place, the rite begins in the first room visited with the antiphon and concludes in the last room visited with the concluding prayer.

In the first instance, when all have gathered, the rite may be expanded by using elements form the rite for Communion in Ordinary Circumstances, such as a reading from Scripture and a brief reflection on the reading. The pastoral minister will need to judge what is the most appropriate and practical manner to use this rite, keeping in mind that the intention is to avoid any semblance of expediency or minimalist ritual.

> In brining communion to them the minister of communion represents Christ and manifests faith and charity on behalf of the whole community toward those who cannot be present at the eucharist.
>
> —*Pastoral Care of the Sick*, 73

Outline of the Rite

Introductory Rite

- Antiphon

Liturgy of Holy Communion

- Greeting
- The Lord's Prayer
- Communion

Concluding Rite

- Concluding Prayer

---

17. See PCS, 78.

Create a prayerful environment including linens, a crucifix, and the pyx.

Although a priest or deacon can lead this rite, the rubrics seem to suggest a lay pastoral minister in this role. The rite begins with one of the three antiphons in the text. If the minister moves from room to room another person may accompany them with a lighted candle. The minister will need to check with the residence manager to make sure that an open flame is allowed.

Upon entering each room the minister offers a greeting from the two options. The second option is the same as the one used by the priest at Mass. However, the one in the ritual text uses the former translation. The minister might want to insert the new translation in his or her ritual text. The pyx or ciborium with the Blessed Sacrament is then placed on a table and "all join in adoration."[18] At this point it is appropriate to have a reading from Scripture. The suggested options are those in the ritual text from Communion of the Sick in Ordinary Circumstances[19] or from those listed in the appendix of the rite. The rubrics note that the reading is included "if there is time and it seems desirable."[20] The time factor might depend on how many communicants there are; the "desirable" factor might depend on the ability of the sick person to be attentive. Once again, the rite envisions a full prayer experience for the sick, and by inference, discourages short cuts. At the same time, the minister can make adaptations that better suit the particular situation of each person.

At this point in the rite the Lord's Prayer is said, "when circumstances permit."[21] One example of such a circumstance is when there are only a few rooms to visit. The recitation of the Lord's Prayer does not seem to be an onerous expectation, and being able to include the sick person in this rite

---

18. PCS, 93.
19. See PCS, 84.
20. PCS, 93.
21. PCS, 93.

outweighs the pressure of time. The minister might arrange his or her schedule to allow for whatever time it takes to do this good ministry.

The minister gives Communion in the usual way, noting that the words in the two options used as the host is shown to the person are different from those used at Mass. If there are others in attendance they may also receive Communion. The rubrics make no mention of Communion in the form of the Precious Blood in this rite.

The concluding prayer is said in the last room that is visited, or in the place where all are gathered, such as a chapel, if that is the arrangement. One can imagine a variation on the arrangement in a hospital or institutional setting. It's possible that a number of residents are able to gather in a chapel or suitable common room, and that there are some who are unable to join them and remain in their rooms. In this case, additional ministers can take Communion to the individual rooms while the minister gives Communion to the others. The ministers who visit the sick in their rooms should at least offer a greeting when they arrive, recite the Lord's Prayer, and conclude with suitable words of farewell. The rubrics state that a final blessing is not given, which seems unusual, especially when several communicants gather in a common space. This is a good time to include a chant or hymn, if the minister is capable of doing so.

The liturgical environment for this rite will depend on the arrangement in the hospital, institution, or residence. The chapel setting will have the necessary liturgical furnishings and seasonal décor. It seems unlikely that anything else will need to be added for this simple rite. The individual rooms should have a table on which to place the Blessed Sacrament; if none are available, the minister simply holds the pyx or ciboria. If the minister has an assistant for the room visits then that person could carry a corporal from room to room.

Chapter 4: Anointing of the Sick

The post-conciliar rite for the Sacrament of the Anointing of the Sick "provides the Church with a model for celebrating the mystery of God's healing power as it confronts human illness and the mystery of suffering."[22] The theological shift from preparing for death to healing is clearly embedded in the elements of the rite. The rite "mirrors the mystery of God's life-saving

---

22. Dennis C. Smolarski, sj, *Sacred Mysteries: Sacramental Principles and Liturgical Practice* (New York, NY: Paulist Press, 1995) 99.

love that triumphs over human weakness, even over death. Ultimately the sacrament is a celebration of the Paschal Mystery of Christ's death and resurrection, of new life through suffering and death."[23]

In the celebration of the sacrament, the Church "supports the sick in their struggle against illness and continues Christ's messianic work of healing."[24] The ecclesial character of the sacrament is expressed in the ministry of those who care for the sick, in the prayers of the community for the sick, and in the gestures and words of the priest. "When the priest anoints the sick, he is anointing in the name and with the power of Christ himself (see Mark 6:13)."[25] By virtue of Baptism all members of the Body of Christ share in the suffering of Christ and of the members of his Body, the Church.

The sacrament of anointing is the proper sacrament for those Christians whose health is seriously impaired by sickness or old age.

—*Pastoral Care of the Sick*, 97

There are three distinct and integral elements in the celebration of the Sacrament of the Anointing of the Sick: the prayer of faith, the laying on of hands, and the anointing with blessed oil.[26] The prayer of faith is the action of the whole community of believers, represented in the actual celebration by the priest and those who are in attendance. The laying on of hands has its roots in the actions of Jesus who reached out to touch those who came to him for healing.[27] In the celebration of the sacrament the gesture of the priest echoes this action of Christ and indicates that the person who is sick is the concern of Christ and his Church. The laying on of hands is a sign of blessing and it is done in silence. The anointing with oil is another expression of the Church's continuing ministry of Christ.[28] The gesture of touch expresses comfort and concern for the sick person and echoes the use of oil for soothing pain and strengthening the body.

Chapter 4 of the ritual text includes three rites for use in different circumstances. Each rite allows for adaptations depending on pastoral circumstances.

---

23. Smolarski, 99.
24. PCS, 98.
25. PCS, 98.
26. See PCS, 105, 106, and 107.
27. See Luke 4:40.
28. See Mark 6:13.

Anointing outside Mass

Outline of the Rite

Introductory Rites

- Greeting
- Sprinkling with Holy Water
- Instruction
- Penitential Act

Liturgy of the Word

- Reading
- Response

Liturgy of Anointing

- Litany
- Laying On of Hands
- Prayer over the Oil
- Anointing
- Prayer after Anointing
- The Lord's Prayer

[Liturgy of Holy Communion]

- Communion
- Silent Prayer
- Prayer after Communion

Concluding Rite

- Blessing

The Rite of Anointing outside Mass is in the context of a Liturgy of the Word and can be celebrated in a home, a health care setting, such as a hospital, or in the church. The Communion Rite is optional. One or more persons may be anointed during the celebration of the rite and other persons may assist. If the anointing takes place in a home then a suitable table should be provided for the vessel of oil, the ritual book, one or two candles, and a bowl of water (with a lemon wedge), and a small towel for the priest to wash his hands after the anointing(s). The priest should vest for this liturgy of anointing. If the rite takes place in a hospital or other institutional setting then the same items need to be available. A lectern could be used for the Lectionary; sheets of paper should never be used for reading the Word of God. If the rite takes place in the church, these items will be readily available. If other priests are present, because of a large number of sick persons to be anointed, then sufficient vessels are needed for the holy oil. Additional priests should also be vested in alb and stole. The color choice for the stole may be white, or the color of the liturgical season.

Although the priest presides for the rite, a deacon or pastoral minister may assist with the readings and the intercessions. If a large number of people are present, whether in the church or an institution, then it will be both helpful and hospitable to have one or more ministers of hospitality present. They will assist both the sick and their friends and family members with seating arrangements, and with any worship aids that might be used for the liturgy.

Because of its very nature as a sign, the sacrament . . . should be celebrated with members of the family and other representatives of the Christian community.

—*Pastoral Care of the Sick*, 99

The person who coordinates this celebration should invite any health care providers who are free to participate. Their presence is a sign that the sacramental understanding of anointing includes both the physical and the spiritual effects of healing.

The pastoral notes strongly recommend the use of music, especially when there is a large congregation. "The full participation of those present must be fostered by every means, especially through the use of appropriate songs, so that the celebration manifests the Easter joy which is proper to this sacrament."[29] Even unaccompanied chants for the response in the Penitential Act and for the litany are appropriate. The assembly could also be invited to sing during the Communion Rite when it is included in the celebration. An opening and closing hymn is also appropriate. If the anointing takes place in church, the use of music seems expected. Anytime the faithful gather for a communal celebration of the sacraments, the inclusion of music enhances the experience of prayer.

The order of the rite is the same whether there is only one person to be anointed or several. The priest greets the sick person(s) and others who are present using one of the four options in the rite. The rubrics note that he

---

29. PCS, 108.

The Rite of Anointing outside Mass may be celebrated in a home, health care facility, the church, or another appropriate place.

"may" use one of the options,[30] leaving the priest to use other words. If Communion is to be given during the rite the priest places the Blessed Sacrament on a table "and all join in adoration."[31] There is no indication whether this involves any gesture, such as kneeling or genuflection; no words are given so it can be assumed that adoration is done with a moment of silence.

Sprinkling with holy water is optional; if it is done it is accompanied by one of three acclamations. If the rite is celebrated with a number of people in an institutional setting or in the church, the priest should include all present in the sprinkling rite.

Following the sprinkling rite the priest gives an instruction. He reminds everyone that they are gathered in the name of Christ and he recalls the words from the letter of the Apostle James (5:13–15). He invites everyone to pray for the sick person(s), thereby expressing the importance of the prayer of faith in the celebration of the sacrament.

If the person to be anointed wishes to celebrate the Sacrament of Penance at this time, the Rite for Reconciliation of Individual Penitents is used. If there are several persons to be anointed and wish to celebrate the Sacrament of Penance at this liturgy be sure to have additional priests on hand. Otherwise, arrangements should be made to provide the Sacrament of Penance at another time. If the Sacrament of Penance is celebrated within the rite then the Penitential Act is omitted.

---

30. See PCS, 115 and 81.
31. PCS, 115.

When the Penitential Act is used there are three options: the Confiteor, though the former translation is provided in the text; and two variations of the Kyrie with tropes.

The Word of God consists of one reading taken from those in the rite or from the appendix. Either the priest or another person proclaims the reading from Scripture. After a short period of silence, the priest may offer a brief reflection on how the Scripture applies to the needs of the sick and keeping in mind the ability of the sick person to be attentive.

—●●—

> The readings and the homily should help those present to reach a deeper understanding of the mystery of human suffering in relation to the paschal mystery of Christ.
>
> —*Pastoral Care of the Sick*, 100

The liturgy of anointing begins with a litany. Several intercessions are offered, although these may be shortened, depending on the condition of the sick.[32] At that point the priest lays his hands on the head of the sick person in silence. There follows a prayer over the oil. If the oil has been blessed then the prayer is in the form of thanksgiving. Everyone is invited to say the response to each of the invocations with these words, "Blessed be God who heals us in Christ."[33] These words clearly express the understanding that it is God who heals us, and that the Church in her sacramental ministry is the vehicle of God's mercy and providence. If the oil has not been blessed, then the priest uses the prayer of blessing or one of the options found in the rite.[34] Normally, the oil would have been blessed by the bishop at the Chrism Mass on or near Holy Thursday. The oil used for anointing is olive oil; however, "other oil derived from plants" can be used if olive oil is difficult to obtain.[35]

There follows the actual anointing of the sick person(s). They are anointed on the forehead and on the hands. The formula is said in two parts: first on the forehead, "Through this holy anointing / may the Lord in his love and mercy help you / with the grace of the Holy Spirit"; then on the hands, "May the Lord who frees you from sin / save you and raise you up."[36]

---

32. See PCS, 121.
33. PCS, 123.
34. See PCS, 139 or 248.
35. PCS, 20.
36. PCS, 124.

This formula for anointing clearly and succinctly expresses the rich theology of the sacrament. The words for anointing clearly express the healing intent of the sacrament. It is the grace of the Lord, through the action of the Holy Spirit, that brings healing to the sick person. There is no mention of preparation for dying or for entering into eternal life. The hope is that the sick person will be well again, in body and spirit, and that they will be raised up by the power of the

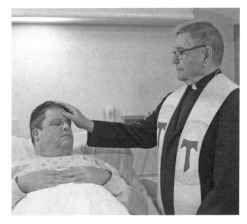

Anointing gives the person hope of recovery in body and spirit.

Lord and the grace of the Holy Spirit. The rite is obviously not the "Last Rite" as the second part of the prayer asks the Lord to raise up the sick person. Unlike the form for anointing in the rite of 1964, the revised rite uses the language of resurrection and new life.[37] The intention is to give hope to the sick person that they will be restored to a new life beyond their current state.

The rubrics suggest that other parts of the body may be anointed, particularly the area of pain or injury. However, the rubrics caution that this is done "depending upon the culture and traditions of the place, as well as the condition of the sick person."[38] No example is given in the rite as to what these cultural issues or traditions might be. The sick person may consider that touching other parts of the body to be inappropriate. On the other hand, an older person may remember the tradition called for several anointings and request the anointing of the senses. In any case, if the priest is not sure, then he should ask before proceeding. If additional anointings are done, the formula is not repeated.

After the anointing the priest says a prayer that addresses the situation of the sick person. He chooses from two for general illness, which could be used when there are several who have been anointed; or from one of the following: in extreme or terminal illness, in advanced age, before surgery, for a child, for a young person. The Lord's Prayer is said, and if those who have been

---

37.   The formula for anointing in the 1964 rite, which maintained the focus on the forgiveness of sins found in the Roman Ritual of 1614, was "May the Lord forgive you by this holy anointing and his most loving mercy whatever sins you have committed by the use of your sight. Amen." The formula was repeated over each of the five senses, plus on the feet.

38.   PCS, 124.

anointed are to receive Communion, the Rite of Communion is celebrated. If there is a large number of people present then other priests or other ministers may assist with the Communion Rite. If some of the sick have difficulty approaching the table or the altar then assistants can direct the Communion ministers to their places. Any others who have gathered for this celebration may receive Communion. After Communion, a brief period of silence is observed and the rite concludes with the Prayer after Communion; three options are provided. The rite provides four options for the final blessing. The first three have four intercessions; the fourth one is a single sentence.

Anointing within Mass

The celebration of anointing within Mass seems most suited to a large gathering of persons in a suitable place within an institution or in the church. However, the pastoral notes do not rule out using this rite in a person's home. The permission of the bishop is not required if the celebration takes place outside the church since canon 932 allows for Mass to take place outside of a sacred space if necessity warrants this situation.

Other large gatherings envisioned by the rite include a diocesan celebration for the sick, a parish wide celebration for its members who are sick, the members of a society for the sick, or during a pilgrimage. If some of the sick wish to celebrate the Sacrament of Penance then that should happen before Mass begins.

There are two pastoral situations to be considered when the Anointing of the Sick takes place within Mass. One is the celebration of the ritual Mass for the Sick.[39] When this Mass is celebrated the proper prayers are taken from Masses and Prayers for Various Needs and Occasions.[40] This liturgy is one that is specifically prepared and celebrated for the sick and the prayers, readings, and music are chosen with the sick in mind. For this liturgy, the priest wears white vestments.[41]

> The full participation of those present must be fostered by every means, especially through the use of appropriate songs, so that the celebration manifests the Easter joy which is proper to this sacrament.
>
> —*Pastoral Care of the Sick*, 100

---

39. See *The Roman Missal*, Ritual Masses, For the Conferral of the Anointing of the Sick, II.
40. See *The Roman Missal*, Masses for Various Needs and Occasions, For the Sick, 45.
41. Note that there are restrictions as to when the ritual Mass of the sick can be celebrated; see PCS, 134.

Celebrating the Anointing of the Sick at Mass seems more appropriate if there are larger numbers of people seeking the sacrament.

A second scenario is when the Anointing of the Sick takes place during the Sunday Eucharist and without changing the proper prayers or the readings designated for that Sunday. This latter situation has become a common practice in parishes and is often scheduled one or more times during the year.

Outline of the Rite

Introductory Rites

- Greeting
- Reception of the Sick
- Penitential Act
- Collect

Liturgy of the Word

Liturgy of Anointing

- Litany
- Laying On of Hands
- Prayer over the Oil
- Anointing
- Prayer after Anointing

Liturgy of the Eucharist

Concluding Rites

- Blessing

- Dismissal

With a few exceptions, this order of the rite is similar to the rite for anointing outside of Mass. After the initial liturgical greeting the priest addresses those who have gathered with words of welcome to the sick, assuring them that Christ is present to them and cares for them. The Penitential Act is omitted. The rite itself provides two options for the collect and the Liturgy of the Word proceeds in the usual manner. If this celebration is a ritual Mass for the Sick the readings are chosen from the *Lectionary for Mass*.[42] In his homily, the priest or deacon should relate the Scripture texts to the Christian understanding of illness and the relationship between human sickness and divine grace that comes to the sick in the Sacrament of Anointing. When parishes schedule Anointing of the Sick during a Sunday liturgy, the readings of that Sunday should lend themselves to a reflection on the meaning of human suffering and the power of God to raise us up to new life through the grace of the sacrament. This message is surely appropriate for those who healthy as well as those who are sick.

The Universal Prayer is omitted since petitions are included in the litany. This applies both in the ritual Mass for the Sick and at a Sunday Mass when Anointing of the Sick is celebrated.

The Liturgy of Anointing begins with a Litany, followed by the laying on of hands in silence. If there is a large number of sick to be anointed, and if there are several priests present, then the laying on of hands should include each person who is to be anointed. Although the rubrics don't offer an exception to the individual gesture, the actual situation may pose a difficulty for this to happen in a timely manner. The rite clearly envisions the laying on of hands for each person in order to preserve the biblical tradition of this gesture and to express the tender love of Christ himself for each person.[43]

There follows the prayer over the oil, either in thanksgiving or as a blessing, similar to the rite of anointing outside Mass. The two-part formula for anointing is used; the forehead and the hands of each sick person are anointed. It should be noted here that the rubrics don't indicate the manner of the

---

42. See LM, 790–795,

43. See PCS, 139.

When Anointing takes place at Mass, the Liturgy of the Eucharist occurs in the usual way.

anointing. One might think that the blessed oil is applied using the form of the cross, as with the mark of ashes, but that is not specified. Usually the priest applies the oil by rubbing the forehead and hands with the ends of his fingers, as though massaging the skin. The gesture is brief but should be done in such a way that the person feels the touch and the impression of oil upon their body. Contrary to the rite of 1964 that called for the oil to be immediately wiped off with a cotton swab, there is no such requirement in the revised rite.

When all the sick have been anointed, the priest says one of the prayers in the rite. If several persons have been anointed then one of the two "general" options are used. If only one person has been anointed then the priest may choose one of the general prayers, or the one for "Extreme or Terminal Illness" or the one for "Advanced Age."[44]

The Liturgy of the Eucharist continues in the usual way; the rite provides a proper Preface. There are three embolisms that can be added to Eucharist Prayer I, II, or III. These insertions make specific reference to the presence of the sick in the assembly and express the sense that they are an integral part of the Church at prayer. The two options for the Prayer after Communion speak of healing as a gift of God. The Concluding Rite borrows two blessings from the Rite of Anointing outside Mass; each has four

44.   PCS, 142.

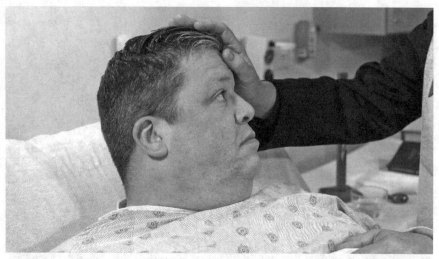

When anointing takes place in the hospital, the person is not considered to be in imminent danger of death; otherwise, Viaticum would be given.

invocations with the response "Amen." A short form of the blessing is also provided. There are no words of dismissal in the ritual text. It seems appropriate that the priest or deacon supply the words and, at the suggestion of the rubric, commend the sick to the care of those who have gathered with them.[45]

Anointing in a Hospital or Institution

This third Rite of Anointing is designed for those situations in which only the priest and the sick person are present. Although it is an abbreviated rite it retains the essential elements of the Sacrament of Anointing. The physical setting that is mentioned in the introduction includes an emergency room or casualty ward of a hospital. However, the person to be anointed is not considered to be in imminent danger of death. If that were the case then Viaticum would be the appropriate sacrament. If the physical and/or the medical circumstances make it difficult to celebrate the rite, and if the person is not in danger of dying, then the priest should wait until the setting is more amenable for anointing.

Outline of the Rite

Introductory Rites

- Greeting
- Instruction

---

45. See PCS, 148.

Liturgy of Anointing

- Laying On of Hands

- Anointing

- The Lord's Prayer

- Prayer after Anointing

Concluding Rite

- Blessing

A simple greeting begins the Rite of Anointing, although the priest might take a few moments to make sure that the sick person is aware of their situation and offer words of comfort and encouragement. A short instruction that includes the text from the Letter of the Apostle James is given and a opening prayer follows. The laying on of hands is done in silence and then the priest anoints the person in the usual way with the twofold formula. The same rubrics concerning additional anointings is included in this rite as well.[46] The Lord's Prayer is said, and if the sick person is able, they join in. The prayer after anointing is chosen from those in the ritual text for the first form of the rite.[47] In order to choose the prayer that would be best suited to the sick person, the priest should inquire beforehand as to the condition of the person. A final blessing concludes the rite.

As part of his pastoral ministry the priest should inquire about what, if any, pastoral care is in place for the

> Through this holy anointing
> may the Lord in his love and mercy
> help you
> with the grace of the Holy Spirit.
> Amen.
>
> —*Pastoral Care of the Sick*, 124

person who has been anointed, and if needed, make the necessary arrangements for that to happen. In such a situation the priest acts as an advocate for the sick, either with the pastoral care ministers in the parish or with the appropriate health care providers.

Part 2: Pastoral Care of the Dying

Part 2 of *Pastoral Care of the Sick* includes four rites to assist the Church in her ministry of comfort and prayer to those who are dying: The Celebration

---

46. See PCS, 157.
47. See PCS, 159 and 125.

of Viaticum; the Commendation of the Dying; Prayers for the Dead; and Rites for Exceptional Circumstances. The first three rites found in chapters 5, 6, and 7 are intended for use in "those situations in which time is not a pressing concern and the rites can be celebrated fully and properly."[48] The Rites for Exceptional Circumstances in chapter 8 are used in those "emergency situations sometimes encountered in the ministry to the dying."[49]

Although priests in pastoral leadership have the first responsibility for the care of the dying, they should be assisted by other pastoral ministers, as well as family, friends, and health care providers. With the exception of the Celebration of Viaticum within Mass, other pastoral ministers, including deacons and lay ministers, may preside at the rites for the dying. The larger community of faith also shares in this ministry by attending to the dying, when appropriate, and holding them in prayer.

Chapter 5: Celebration of Viaticum

There are two rites for the celebration of Viaticum, one within Mass and one outside of Mass. Within the post-Conciliar liturgical rites, the celebration of Viaticum is seen as the proper sacrament for a person who is dying. The word *viaticum* reveals the intent of the sacrament. *Viaticus* refers to the "taking of a journey" and the ancient custom of providing a meal before embarking on the journey.[50] In the early history of the Church, *viaticum* had a broader meaning as being the food for the journey of life. Over time, the Eucharist as Viaticum came to be understood as the source of strength and comfort for those at the end of their earthly journey and prepared them to enter their journey to a new life with God.[51] An eighth-century sacramentary directed that an account of the Passion of the Lord be read before the dying person received Communion. Thus, the dying person "was prepared for death from both the table of the word and the table of the

> The Christian community has a continuing responsibility to pray for and with the person who is dying. Through its sacramental ministry to the dying the community helps Christians to embrace death in mysterious union with the crucified and risen Lord, who awaits them in the fullness of life.
>
> —*Pastoral Care of the Sick*, 16

---

48. PCS, 161.
49. PCS, 161.
50. See Gusmer, 107.
51. See Gusmer, 108.

Eucharist."[52] Although Viaticum was celebrated for the dying during this period, it was not the last sacrament. The popularity of death-bed confessions, which necessitated the presence of a priest, and the understanding that anointing, which also required the presence of a priest, meant that these two sacraments were frequently celebrated *after* Viaticum. This order of the sacraments, with the understanding that anointing was the immediate preparation for death, was maintained until the revised rite of the Second Vatican Council of 1972.

Viaticum within Mass

Outline of the Rite

Introductory Rites
Liturgy of the Word

- Readings

- Homily

- Baptismal Profession of Faith

- Litany

Liturgy of the Eucharist

- Sign of Peace

- Communion as Viaticum

Concluding Rites

- Blessing

- [Apostolic Pardon]

- Dismissal

The celebration of *Viaticum* within Mass may take place in the person's home or in a health care facility. The rite envisions that a full celebration of Mass take place, but allows that circumstances may be such that the rite for *Viaticum* outside Mass is more appropriate. Examples of these circumstances might be the imminent death of the person and/or the lack of a suitable space within an institution. Even if Mass is celebrated the rite may be shortened if it seems appropriate. For example, only one Scripture reading may be used, though it should be a gospel passage.

---

52. Gusmer, 110.

> Priests and other ministers entrusted with the spiritual care of the sick should do everything they can to ensure that those in proximate danger of death receive the body and blood of Christ as viaticum.
>
> —*Pastoral Care of the Sick*, 176

The liturgical environment is, out of necessity, relatively simple. A table with a white cloth is needed, as well as a lighted candle (if possible), a pyx large enough for extra hosts if other people are present and intend to receive Communion, a chalice and purificator, the ritual text for Viaticum, and *The Roman Missal*. The priest should "wear attire appropriate to this ministry."[53]

The rite does not provide rubrics for the opening greeting or the Penitential Act. If the person wishes to receive the Sacrament of Penance, that can take place before Mass begins. In that case the Penitential Act could be omitted. However, the rubrics suggest that it would be preferable for the Sacrament of Penance to be celebrated at another time prior to the celebration of Viaticum.[54] It is assumed that there is a formal greeting, as with any celebration of Mass, followed by a Penitential Act. The Collect, Prayer over the Offerings, and the Prayer after Communion are taken from the Mass for the Administering of Viaticum.[55]

After the Gospel the priest may give a "brief homily on the sacred text in which he explains the meaning and importance of *Viaticum*."[56] A homily is optional, perhaps in consideration of the condition of the person who is dying. If one is given, the catechetical nature of the homily may be for the benefit of those accompanying the dying person, as well as the person who is dying. In any case, brevity is called for.

One of the distinctive elements in this rite is the renewal of the baptismal Profession of Faith which follows the homily. The rubrics note that this is done "if the sick person is to renew his or her baptismal profession of faith."[57] Since it is unlikely that the person knows that this is an option for the Profession of Faith (the Creed), then the priest should explain why this is appropriate. He should draw the connection between the baptismal promises

---

53. PCS, 177. The pastoral notes don't state what attire is appropriate. One could assume that the priest wears at least an alb and stole, definitely not a stole over street clothes. A chasuble is always expected for the celebration of Mass, though it might be optional in this situation.

54. See PCS, 185.

55. See *The Roman Missal*, Ritual Masses, Mass for Administering Viaticum, III.

56. PCS, 189.

57. PCS, 190.

at the time of Baptism when the sick person was baptized into the death and Resurrection of Christ and their present situation of preparing to enter the fullness of the Paschal Mystery. This explanation should emphasize the sense of Christian hope that all have of being with God, and the joy that awaits all of us when we are welcomed into eternal life. The priest will want to avoid any pious comments that mask the reality of death or ignore the lived faith of the person who is dying.

After the Profession of Faith, in either form, there is a short litany. It resembles the Universal Prayer and may be shortened or omitted if the person has made a Profession of Faith or if they appear to be tiring.[58] If other ministers or family members are present, they could read the intercessions.

The Liturgy of Eucharist proceeds as usual. The rubrics note that the Sign of Peace may be given to the sick person at the usual place. The Communion Rite takes place as usual; both the Body and Blood of Christ are offered to the sick person, and to others who are present and wish to receive. In place of the formula, "Behold the Lamb of God" the words for Viaticum may be used: "Jesus Christ is the food for our journey; he calls us to the heavenly table" or "These are God's holy gifts to his holy people: receive them with thanksgiving."[59] Immediately after giving Communion to the sick person the priest adds: "May the Lord Jesus Christ protect you and lead you to eternal life."[60]

The rite offers three options for the blessing at the end of Mass. The words of the first two options speak of comfort and strength for the sick person, reflecting once again the concern of the Church for the sick and the firm belief that their life and their death is in the hands of a loving and merciful God. Before the dismissal the priest may impart an Apostolic Pardon.[61]

Viaticum outside Mass

Outline of the Rite
Introductory Rites
- Greeting
- Sprinkling with Holy Water

---

58.   See PCS, 191.

59.   PCS, 193.

60.   PCS, 193.

61.   An Apostolic Pardon is a blessing to which a plenary indulgence is attached, given before death for the remission of the temporal punishment due to sin. It is given in danger-of-death situations, usually with the reception of the Sacraments of Reconciliation and Viaticum.

- Instruction
- Penitential Rite
- [Apostolic Pardon]

Liturgy of the Word

- Reading
- Homily
- Baptismal Profession of Faith
- Litany

Liturgy of Viaticum

- The Lord's Prayer
- Communion as Viaticum
- Silent Prayer
- Prayer after Communion

Concluding Rites

- Blessing
- Sign of Peace

"Although viaticum celebrated in the context of the full Eucharistic celebration is always preferable, when it is not possible the rite for Viaticum outside Mass is appropriate."[62] In order to emphasize that the sacraments are intended to be communal acts of worship, this rite should, if circumstances allow, be celebrated with other persons present. Family members, care givers, members of the local faith community, and friends of the dying could be invited to participate. The priest who has responsibility for pastoral care, as well as members of the liturgy team, pastoral visitors, and the person who is sick should be involved in preparing for the celebration. Recall that this rite and the Rite for Viaticum within Mass are celebrated when the condition of the sick person is relatively stable, even though there is the very real possibility of their impending death. If it is an emergency situation then the rite for emergencies is celebrated.[63] However, this rite may be abbreviated if the condition of the sick person is a concern.

---

62. PCS, 186.
63. See PCS, 264–274.

A priest, deacon, or lay pastoral minister may preside at this rite. The priest or deacon should be vested in an alb and stole. The lay pastoral minister is not required to vest, although they could wear an alb. If the sick person is not going to celebrate the Sacrament of Penance or Anointing, then a deacon or lay pastoral minister may preside.

The rite begins with the usual greeting; although given the nature of the situation the minister should begin in an informal way so that everyone is at ease and any update on the condition of the sick person is taken into consideration. If the sick person wishes to celebrate the Sacrament of Penance before Viaticum, this can be done during an earlier visit. The pastoral notes accompanying the rite should be observed and if it is part of this visit then the Penitential Act is omitted.[64]

The rite gives the option for sprinkling with holy water after the initial greeting. A short acclamation is said. The minister then offers a brief introduction, using the one given in the ritual text or using his or her own words.[65] If the Sacrament of Penance is not celebrated then the Penitential Act is included. Two forms are given: the Confiteor, although the one in the text is the former translation, and one with three tropes with response. The rite provides the option of the Apostolic Pardon at this point.[66]

The Liturgy of the Word can include one or more readings, although the rubrics indicate only one reading. The reading can be selected from the four offered in the rite, or from the options provided in the appendix of the ritual text. A person, other than the minister, can proclaim the Scripture reading. A brief homily can be given, though the minister needs to be conscious of the ability of the sick person to be attentive for any period of time. The Profession of Faith takes the form of the renewal of baptismal promises, but only using the last three questions pertaining to belief. The first three concerning the rejection of the ways of the devil are omitted.

The litany is in the form of intercessory prayer; three intercessions are given. The number may be more or less, depending on the condition of the sick person, If the person is tiring, and they have made a profession of faith, then the litany may be omitted altogether. The Liturgy of Viaticum follows the same order as that celebrated with Mass. As with the celebration of Viaticum within Mass, the rite provides for Communion under both kinds.

---

64. The rite for the celebration of Penance in this situation is outlined in PCS, 299–305.
65. See PCS, 199.
66. See page 63 for a description of the Apostolic Pardon.

This requires that the minister make suitable arrangements to carry the Precious Blood to the place of the celebration. In practice, this is more often the exception. Any of those who are present may also receive Communion at this time. A moment of silence is observed after Communion. This has a twofold purpose. It allows the sick person to renew their attentiveness and it allows others to reflect on the wonderful gift of the Eucharist and the grace that the Lord bestows on all who are in Communion with him and with each other, especially at a time of human suffering.

The rite offers a concluding prayer from four options. The Prayer after Communion from the Mass for the Administering of Viaticum might be used here, but it seems more practical to use one from the rite since there would be no other reason to bring *The Roman Missal* for this celebration. The concluding rites include three options for the blessing. If the minister is not a priest or a deacon, then a different form is used as he or she makes the Sign of the Cross on themselves and invokes a blessing on all who are present. If the minister is a priest or deacon, and if one or more consecrated hosts remain, then he uses the pyx to impart the blessing.

At the end of the rite the Sign of Peace may be exchanged with the sick person and with those who have assembled for the celebration. If it seems desirable, and if the minister is able, it would be appropriate for a sung chant or hymn to conclude the rite.

Chapter 6: Commendation of the Dying

Chapter 6 in the *Pastoral Care of the Sick* does not provide a particular rite, but offers a number of prayers and Scripture texts for commendation of the dying. These resources are organized by the following six groups:

- Short Texts from Scripture
- Readings from Scripture
- Litany of the Saints
- Prayers of Commendation
- Prayers after Death
- Prayers for the Family and Friends

There is no particular order for using the prayers or the Scripture passages; the priest, deacon, or lay minister may choose as many or as few as seem appropriate in any given pastoral situation. Additional readings from Scripture are also available in the appendix of the ritual text.

The pastoral notes for this chapter emphasize the responsibility of the Church to accompany those who are dying by being present to them, praying for and with them, offering encouragement to them, and comfort to their family and friends. The time of death is especially difficult for those who are close to the dying person and the Church reaches out to them, as well as to the dying, with every kindness and solicitude. Other members of the community of faith are encouraged to be present to the dying, keeping in mind the need for the immediate family to spend these precious moments of life with their loved one.

> The dying person and all who are present may receive communion under both kinds. The sign of communion is more complete when received in this manner because it expresses more fully and more clearly the nature of the eucharist as meal, one which prepares all who take part in it for the heavenly banquet.
>
> —*Pastoral Care of the Sick*, 181

The presence of the priest or pastoral care minister reassures the dying and the family members that the Church cares deeply for all her flock, and in a very special way, for those who are suffering or hurting as death approaches. The rubrics indicate an awareness of the fragile nature of this time and suggest that the prayers be said "in a slow, quiet voice, alternating with periods of silence."[67] In some situations, the moment of death arrives after a period of unconsciousness. Even while a person is unconscious, prayers can be said so that those who are present can be given a sense of comfort, and can become aware of a connection with the dying as they prepare to enter communion with the Risen Lord. The dying person may be blessed with holy water and those present can be invited to hold the hands of the dying or to trace the cross on their forehead. The sense of touch may still be detected by the dying person and provide an unknown comfort. If the person dies while the minister is still present, he or she moves to the Prayers after Death. Although the rubrics state that "immediately"[68] after death has occurred these prayers are said, it seems pastorally advisable that a few moments elapse so that any family members who are present have time to compose themselves. One of the traits of a good pastoral minister is being aware of the

---

67. PCS, 214.
68. PCS, 216.

emotions of those who accompany the sick and the dying. There is no need for a hurried approach. When someone dies the world of those who remain comes to a stop. Some will feel paralyzed, others will be distraught, others may be angry. Once there seems to be some calm and at least a hesitant acceptance of death, then additional prayers can be said.

Chapter 7: Prayers for the Dead

Outline of the Rite

- Greeting
- Prayer
- Reading
- Litany
- The Lord's Prayer
- Prayer of Commendation

Chapter 7 in the *Pastoral Care of the Sick* is intended for use by the pastoral minister who is asked to attend to a "person who is already dead."[69] The prayers that are provided come from two sources, those that are new compositions and those that are taken from the *Order of Christian Funerals*. The latter include the two opening prayers; the prayer that concludes the Litany; and the prayer of Commendation.

One of the questions that arose during the time when the Sacrament of Anointing was called Extreme Unction, and when it was understood to be the sacrament when death was imminent, was at what point did death actually occur. Scholastic theology, which was affirmed by the Council of Trent, was based on the notion that the material and the spiritual were distinct entities within the human person. In practice, this led to an acceptance of dying that first took away physical life and only after spiritual life. The spiritual life was within the soul and since the last rites were to prepare the soul for eternity, then the person could be anointed after physical death had taken place. It was believed that the soul remained in the person for at least an hour, and an anointing could take place within that time. With the reform of the rite of anointing, and a renewed understanding that the sacraments, including anointing, were for the living, this practice changed. In the few years after the reform of the Sacrament of Anointing, even with its new name as the

---

69. PCS, 223.

sacrament of the sick, many faithful found it difficult to understand why a loved one could not be anointed, even though it was obvious that the person was dead. Over time, with careful catechesis, people have come to accept the practice of anointing the sick, and of praying for the dead in those moments immediately after death.

This chapter of the ritual text is a response to that pastoral need. The pastoral notes are actually clear in this regard. "A priest is not to administer the sacraments of penance or anointing"[70] if he is called to attend a person who is dead. If the person dies at home and there is no health care professional present who could make a determination of death, then the priest, in consultation with those who are present, should ascertain, at least by observation, if the person has died. If it is determined that the person is dead, then the priest continues with the Prayers for the Dead.

The pastoral notes give good advice for this situation: "It may be necessary (for the priest) to explain to the family of the person who is dead that the sacraments are celebrated for the living, not for the dead, and that the dead are effectively helped by the prayers of the living."[71]

Since the rituals of the Church always engage those who celebrate them, and since communal prayer is very powerful in its own mysterious way, the act of praying together in this

> Christians have the responsibility of expressing their union in Christ by joining the dying person in prayer for God's mercy and for confidence in Christ.
>
> —*Pastoral Care of the Sick*, 213

situation has a profound effect on the living. In a situation where emotions can be very acute, and arrangements can seem to be somewhat onerous, praying together will be a source of comfort and strength. A good pastoral minister will be aware of the heightened feelings of those present and will lead the prayers with a measured calm. His or her manner and voice can help insert a tone of peace and acceptance at a difficult time.

When it seems appropriate, the minister begins the prayer with a greeting that expresses faith in the mercy of God. Two options are given; the minister may add other words if it seems appropriate. The opening prayer, taken from two that are provided, calls to mind that God's love has always

---

70. PCS, 223.
71. PCS, 224.

been present in the person's life and now they are called to be with God in eternal life.

The rite offers two readings from the Gospel; one from Luke's account of Jesus' own time of dying, and one from John's account of the death and raising of Lazarus. Other options are found in the appendix of the rite.

The Litany of Saints follows the Scripture reading. The rubrics allow for one of the people who are present, besides the minister, to lead this litany. The full form of the litany can be used, or a shorter version, if it seems better suited to the situation. Other names can be added to the litany, including the patron saint of the person, of the parish, and any for whom the deceased had a special devotion.

The litany concludes with a brief prayer followed by the Our Father. The final prayer is the prayer of commendation. The intent of the words in this prayer is to express a form of farewell, a letting go of the earthly life of the person and at the same time making an act of faith in the saving power of Jesus Christ. The prayer petitions the "holy and compassionate" Lord to forgive the sins of the deceased and to welcome them into the "light, joy, and peace of heaven."[72]

The minister may conclude the rite by tracing the Sign of the Cross on the person's forehead. Others may be invited to do the same. A gesture of blessing may also be extended over the body and, if desired, a priest or deacon may sprinkle the body with holy water.[73]

Chapter 8: Rites for Exceptional Circumstances

Chapter 8 of *Pastoral Care of the Sick* offers various rites that can be used in those pastoral situations where the rites outlined above cannot be celebrated in their fullest expression. These rites for exceptional circumstances are provided for use when "there is a genuine necessity, for example, when sudden illness or an accident or some other cause has placed one of the faithful in the proximate or immediate danger of death."[74]

> In its pastoral ministry the Church always seeks to be as complete as possible, and with this continuous rite those who are in danger of death are prepared to face it sustained by all the spiritual means available to the Church.
>
> —*Pastoral Care of the Sick*, 237

---

72. PCS, 231.
73. For additional prayers for the dead, see the *Order of Christian Funerals*, Part V.
74. PCS, 232.

The primary reason for these rites is to ensure that the compassionate ministry of the Church is made available even when an unexpected situation interrupts the normal unfolding of life. In such situations the rituals of the Church, both sacramental and nonsacramental, are celebrated in order that the sick or dying person be held in prayer by the faithful, supported by the presence of the ministers of the Church, and commended to the mercy of Jesus Christ.

The first of two conditions associated with the use of these rites is the sudden and unexpected change in a person's well-being because of a serious accident, a sudden illness—one thinks of a major heart attack—or other incident that precludes a full celebration of the Rite of Anointing or Viaticum. The second condition is the imminent danger of death due to the incident that has taken place. The rites provide adaptations based on the time available, the location of the incident, and the condition of the person. At the same time, the pastoral notes acknowledge that the situation may be of such urgency that the continuous Rite of Penance, Anointing, and Viaticum cannot be celebrated, even in the shorter form provided. In those cases an even shorter order is found in the Rite for Emergencies.

Continuous Rite of Penance, Anointing, and Viaticum

Outline of the Rite

Introductory Rites

- Greeting
- Instruction

Liturgy of Penance

- Sacrament of Penance
- [Penitential Rite]
- [Apostolic Pardon]
- Baptismal Profession of Faith
- Litany

[Liturgy of Confirmation]

- Liturgy of Anointing
- Laying On of Hands
- Prayer over the Oil

- Anointing
- [Prayer after Anointing]

Liturgy of Viaticum
- The Lord's Prayer
- Communion as Viaticum
- Silent Prayer
- Prayer after Communion

Concluding Rites
- Blessing
- Sign of Peace

This rite allows for a single celebration of the three sacraments, and, depending on the circumstances, adaptations can be made in the interest of time and the condition of the person. However, the preference is always that the rite be as complete as possible.[75] Although the rite is under the heading of "Exceptional Circumstances" it is not intended for use at the point of death, but at a time when death would seem to be inevitable but not necessarily imminent. In other words, the person should at least be conscious and aware that the rite is taking place. If at all possible, the person should be encouraged to participate in the rite, if only with a minimum of response. With regard to the person's condition, the pastoral notes make a distinction between "imminent death" and "extreme circumstances." In the former case the Sacrament of Penance is omitted, a single anointing is done, and Viaticum is given. In the latter case, Anointing is omitted and Viaticum is given. In both of these situations the Rite for Emergencies is used.

Since this rite is designed for exceptional circumstances, it can be celebrated wherever the person is located—in a hospital room, a long term care residence, their own home, or some other location where the unexpected incident has taken place. It is unlikely that the person can be moved to the church or even to a chapel, although the latter could be considered. The actual environment for the celebration is very minimal, since allowing for the urgency of the situation is the first concern. The proper minister of the rite

---

75. See PCS, 236.

is a priest, although other ministers and caregivers can be present and can assist with the celebration.

The Introductory Rites are similar to those for the other rites and include an opportunity for the priest to speak to the sick person about the sacraments being celebrated. A short reading from Scripture is proclaimed and the sick person is asked if they wish to celebrate the Sacrament of Penance. If the sick person is not able to make a full confession a "generic" one is allowed[76] and absolution is given. If the Sacrament of Penance is not celebrated then the Penitential Act takes place using one of two options provided. Following the Sacrament of Penance or the Penitential Act, the priest may impart the Apostolic Pardon. The wording of the two options for this pardon are quite different. In the first, the invocation speaks of the "holy mysteries of our redemption" as the source of pardon and God is asked to "release you from all punishment in this life and in the life to come."[77] The pardon is from any remaining punishment due to sin. There is no mention of forgiveness of any sins. The second option is in the form of an absolution. The priest says, "By the authority which the Apostolic See has given me, I grant you a full pardon and the remission of all you sins."[78] In this second formula the priest grants the pardon in light of his authority that comes from the Apostolic See. There is no mention of release from punishment due to sin, as in the first option. The pastoral notes do not explain when one or the other would be used, and what conditions need to exist for the priest to impart the Apostolic Pardon.

There follows the Profession of Faith using the baptismal form with the three questions faith. It seems especially appropriate that there be a connection made to the Sacrament of Baptism at this point. It was in Baptism that the person first entered into the Paschal Mystery, and now as their earthly life draws to a close they are asked to remember the beginning of their life of faith. The priest may sprinkle holy water on the sick person, a gesture that recalls the theology of Baptism found in the writings of St. Paul: "Are you unaware that we who were baptized into Christ Jesus were baptized into his death. We were indeed buried with him through baptism into death, so that,

---

76. PCS, 241.
77. PCS, 243.
78. PCS, 243.

just as Christ was raised from the dead by the glory of the Father, we too might live in newness of life."[79]

A short litany follows the Profession of Faith, and those who are present, as well as the sick person, are invited to respond. Two options are given. The first is similar to a Penitential Act that seeks the mercy of the Lord. The second is in the form of intercessions on behalf of the sick person.

The rite for the Sacrament of Confirmation is given in this section, although it more properly belongs in the rite for initiation of the dying. The pastoral notes state that Confirmation is appropriately celebrated at this point in the Continuous Rite if the person has not been previously confirmed.[80] If the dying person is being initiated into faith with the Sacraments of Baptism, Confirmation, and Eucharist, as would be the case if the sick person is a catechumen, then the Rite of Christian Initiation for the Dying is used.[81] In this continuous rite, the Sacrament of Anointing of the Sick is not celebrated. If the dying person is a baptized Catholic, but has not been confirmed, then the Sacrament of Confirmation may be conferred at this point in the continuous rite. If the dying person is a baptized Christian, but not Catholic, and wishes to be initiated into the Catholic Church, then they may be confirmed, using the Rite of Christian Initiation of the Dying, followed by Viaticum, which would be their first (and possibly last) Communion; but they would not receive the Anointing of the Sick.

If the dying person is a fully initiated Catholic, then the continuous rite proceeds with the Liturgy of Anointing. The priest begins by laying his hands on the sick person in silence. If the oil to be used is not blessed the priest may bless it; if it is already blessed he says the prayer of thanksgiving over the oil.[82] Other blessings are found in the Rite of Anointing within Mass.[83] The anointing takes place in the usual way, using the words associated with two anointings, one on the forehead and one on the hands. If death is imminent, and the condition of the dying person has changed since the beginning of the rite, then one anointing is sufficient and the priest omits the prayer after anointing and immediately gives Viaticum.

The priest begins by inviting the sick person and others who are present to recite the Lord's Prayer. The priest shows the consecrated bread to

---

79. Romans 6:3–4.
80. See PCS, 238.
81. See PCS, 275–296.
82. See PCS, 248.
83. See PCS, 140.

the sick person and recites these words, "Jesus Christ is food for our journey; he calls us to the heavenly table." Or, he may say, "This is the Lamb of God who takes away the sins of the world. Happy are those who are called to his supper." The priest can substitute this second option with the current trans-

—*Pastoral Care of the Sick*, 24

lation in *The Roman Missal*. Others who are present may receive Communion if they wish to do so. If the priest has brought the Precious Blood then the sick person and those present may receive under both kinds. The considerations noted above for the safe transport of the Precious Blood should be observed. After a brief silence the Prayer after Communion is said; two options are provided.

The celebration concludes with one of the blessings. If there are one or more consecrated hosts remaining then the priest uses the pyx as he makes the Sign of the Cross in silence over the sick person. At the end of the celebration the sign of peace is exchanged among those who are present.

If the person recovers, even if they do not return to full health, they should receive additional pastoral care, including a frequent celebration of Viaticum. Just as the pastoral care of the sick and the dying leads to appropriate liturgical celebrations, so too does the liturgy lead to expressions of comfort and accompaniment after the ritual moment has passed.

Rite for Emergencies

The Rite for Emergencies is for use in those situations when "extreme circumstances" preclude even the celebration of the continuous rite described above.[84] The rite is designed to provide "only the barest minimum" of a ritual celebration[85] and at the same time allow the priest to add additional prayers if possible to assist the dying person and those who are present.

The extreme circumstances envisioned by the pastoral notes include a sudden and unexpected danger of death caused by accident or illness, or the inability of the priest to be present until the moments just before the death of the person.

---

84. PCS, 259.
85. PCS, 260.

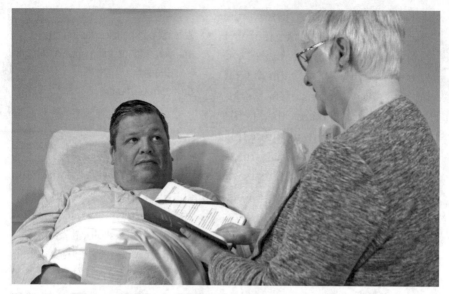

Upon recovery, the person should receive additional pastoral care.

Outline of the Rite

- Sacrament of Penance
- [Apostolic Pardon]
- The Lord's Prayer
- Communion as Viaticum
- [Prayer before Anointing]
- Anointing
- Concluding Prayer
- Blessing
- Sign of Peace

The rite begins by celebrating the Sacrament of Penance if the person wishes to do so. If they are not able to recall all their sins then a generic confession is sufficient. The *Rite of Penance* does not include any exhortation, a prayer of contrition, or act of penance. The formula for absolution is from the *Rite of Penance*. The Apostolic Pardon may be given; the formula given is the first option noted above. There follows the Lord's Prayer.[86] The presider

---

86. Author's note: I have found in my many visits with a person who is dying that even in a weakened state, they will recognize the words of the Lord's Prayer and make every effort to recite it with me and with others who are present.

should be attentive to the person and lead the prayer so that the dying person is able to participate.

Communion as Viaticum is then given, either under both kinds, if possible, or with the Body of Christ. After Communion is given the priest speaks the words of Viaticum, "May the Lord Jesus Christ protect you and lead you to eternal life."[87] As noted above, the priest may omit the prayer before anointing and proceed immediately to the rite of anointing.

If the dying person is not able to celebrate the Sacrament of Penance, and not able to receive Viaticum, the priest may anoint him or her in the usual manner. However, if the person is dead when the priest arrives he is not to perform the Rite of Anointing. He should gently explain the reason for this to those who are present, and assure them that their prayers will accompany the person to the gracious mercy of God.[88] If there is some reason to believe that the person is still living, though nonresponsive, then the priest may anoint conditionally. If he does, then he adds the words "if life is in you" before the anointing.[89]

Once the celebration of the rite has concluded, the priest may wish to lead those present in one or more of the prayers and readings for the Commendation of the Dying.[90] If the person has died before the priest arrives, or dies during his visit, then prayers from Prayers for the Dead can be said.[91] The pastoral care of the family members, friends, and care givers of the deceased person is especially important at this time. Every effort should be made to comfort them and to assist with any concerns they might have or any arrangements they will need to make for the rites of a Christian Funeral.

Christian Initiation for the Dying

The pastoral notes envision that this Rite of Christian Initiation is celebrated for a person who is in danger of death. The rite seems to indicate that there are situations when the dying person is actually able to celebrate the Rite of Christian Initiation of Adults in the normal way, that is, over a period of time and with the other rites associated with full initiation. One thinks of the person who has been diagnosed with a terminal illness and been told that he or she has several months to live. Such a situation allows them to celebrate

---

87. PCS, 267.
88. PCS, 263.
89. PCS, 269.
90. See PCS, 217–222.
91. See PCS, 226–231.

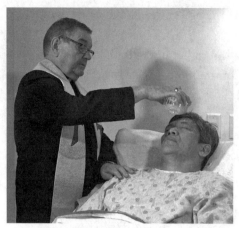

the Rites of Initiation in a more deliberate manner. The Rite for Initiation in this section still assumes that the person, though dying, is able to understand the intent of the rites and capable of participating in them.

If the person is in imminent danger of dying, the short Rite of Baptism is celebrated.

If the person is in imminent danger of dying, whether they are a catechumen or not, then the short Rite for Baptism is celebrated. If the person has been accepted as a catechumen and they recover, then they are to promise to complete the necessary catechesis and the remaining Rites of Initiation.[92] If the person is not a catechumen then they "must give serious indication of being converted to Christ and of renouncing pagan worship, and must not be seen as attached to anything that conflicts with the moral life."[93] If the person or persons who were in proximate danger of death were baptized using the short form for Baptism that only includes the pouring of water and the accompanying words, and they subsequently recover their health, they should receive suitable formation and celebrate the remaining sacraments of initiation.[94]

Outline of the Rite

Introductory Rites
- Greeting
- Dialogue

Liturgy of the Word
- Gospel
- Litany

Liturgy of Christian Initiation
- Renunciation of Sin
- Profession of Faith
- Baptism

---

92. See PCS, 277.
93. PCS, 278.
94. See PCS, 279.

- [Anointing after Baptism]
- [Confirmation]
- The Lord's Prayer
- Communion as Viaticum
- Prayer after Communion

Concluding Rites

- Blessing
- Sign of Peace

The Rite for Christian Initiation for the Dying may take place wherever it is convenient and suitable for the person and those who accompany them. The setting could be a chapel in a hospital or nursing home, the person's own home, or another location that allows for a liturgical celebration. If the person is able, the celebration could take place in his or her parish church. Those in attendance should include family members, godparent(s), any pastoral care visitors that have been visiting the sick person, and any others who are accompanying the person in their time of illness. Water for baptizing, sacred chrism for Confirmation, and the Blessed Sacrament are needed for the celebration. The rite does not call for the use of a white garment or a lighted candle. If the celebration takes place in a chapel or in the church, a candle could be used and lighted from the Paschal candle located there.

As Christ was anointed Priest, Prophet, and King, so may you live always as a member of his body, sharing everlasting life.
Amen.

—Pastoral Care of the Sick, 288

A priest, deacon, or lay person may preside. If a priest is not present, the Sacrament of Confirmation is omitted. There are no suggestions for music during the rite; however, if the celebration takes place in the parish church then one or more hymns could be incorporated in the rite. Those who plan the rite should be conscious of the condition of the sick person in order that the length of the rite not pose a hardship for the person being baptized.

The rite begins with an informal greeting by the minister and a brief conversation about the person's intention and readiness to be baptized. Those who are present are invited to participate in the celebration, assisting the dying person with their presence and their prayers.

The rite provides a formal dialogue in which the minister asks the person about their desire to baptized and their intention to live a Christian life. The godparent(s) and those who are present are asked if they will accept the responsibility of assisting the person in their life as a Christian. The Liturgy of the Word includes at least one reading from the Gospel followed by a brief explanation of the reading. There follows the litany, which is in the form of a series of intercessory prayers. The minister may shorten the litany, depending on the condition of the sick person.

The Liturgy of Initiation begins with the questions of renunciation followed by the questions of faith from the baptismal rite. The last three questions may be replaced by the recitation of the Apostles' Creed. Both options are included in the ritual text. The minister then baptizes the person using the threefold formula. The water need not be blessed. If the minister of the rite is a priest, and the Sacrament of Confirmation is not to be celebrated, then the person is anointed with sacred chrism. If Confirmation is to take place, then the anointing is omitted here and is done during the Liturgy of Confirmation. If the Sacrament of Confirmation is not done, and Viaticum is not given, then the rite concludes with a prayer by the minister, followed by the Our Father and a final blessing.[95]

If a priest is presiding, he confers the Sacrament of Confirmation according to the form in *Pastoral Care of the Sick*, 290–291. There follows a prayer that introduces the Lord's Prayer which all are invited to say together.

The Communion Rite as Viaticum follows the Lord's Prayer and it is celebrated in the same manner as noted above in Viaticum outside of Mass.[96] For the convenience of the one who is presiding, the ritual text repeats the form in this section.[97] If a priest is not presiding at this rite, and the Sacrament of Confirmation is not then conferred, then a deacon or other minister may give Communion as Viaticum.

Care of a Dying Child

In the situation when a child is dying, the Church has a special concern for the pastoral care of the parents and the family. The circumstances and emotions surrounding the imminent death of a child are especially difficult. The priest or pastoral care minister should not attempt to answer all the questions that parents pose at this time; often a ministry of presence can be the most supportive. However, the pastoral minister should continue to accompany the parents after the death of their child with home visits, praying with them and taking up the conversation surrounding a child's death when feelings

---

95. See PCS, 295.
96. See PCS, 297–211.
97. See PCS, 293–296.

Parents may be encouraged to allow the larger faith community to keep the family's needs in prayer. The Universal Prayer is a good option.

are less intense. The parents should be encouraged to let the larger faith community include them in their prayers. Often other parents who have lost a child in death can provide a ministry of consolation that is very comforting for parents at this time.[98]

If a priest or deacon is not available to baptize a child who is dying, then anyone with the intention of the Church "when she baptizes" can do so.[99] In this case, even a nonbaptized person may baptize. If the parents are not able to be present because of the sudden and unexpected circumstances, then the person who baptizes may do so if they reasonably expect that the parents, if otherwise consulted, would consent to have their child baptized.

Pastoral Care of the Sick indicates that if it is possible, the full initiation of a dying child should follow the ritual formulas found in the *Rite for Baptism for Children* and the *Order of Confirmation*.[100] If it is not possible to use the full rites, the formulas provided in *Pastoral Care of the Sick* for emergencies should be used. If the child has reached the age of reason, then they may also receive Communion as Viaticum. If the child does not receive Communion as Viaticum, and they recover from their illness, then they are to complete

---

98. The pastoral notes in PCS,169–172, provide helpful guidelines for pastoral ministers.

99. CCC, 1256.

100. See PCS, 280.

the rites of initiation with the reception of Eucharist and Confirmation "at a fitting time."[101] The Trinitarian formula for Baptism and the pouring of pure water is all that is required for a valid Baptism. This shortened form is used in dire emergencies.

If the child is not in imminent danger of death, and if there is some expectation that the child might regain health, then the child may still be baptized. In this situation, the formulas from the *Rite of Baptism for Children* should be used. If in fact the child regains good health, then the priest or pastoral care minister should encourage the parents to continue the initiation of their child at the appropriate time and with suitable catechesis.

Appendix: Rite for Reconciliation of Individual Penitents

The Rite for Reconciliation of Individual Penitents is found in the appendix of *Pastoral Care of the Sick* and is intended for use in the following situations: during Communion of the Sick, Anointing of the Sick, and Viaticum. These rites have been described previously in this resource and the rubrics for those rites generally apply when using this rite. Since the rite follows the order for the Rite of Reconciliation of Individual Penitents, and since every priest knows that rite from memory, it is hard to imagine when a priest might turn to this rite during a celebration of those rites listed above. Nonetheless, there are a couple of adaptations particular to this rite and noted in the rubrics.

Outline of the Rite
Reception of the Penitent
- Invitation to Trust
- Revelation of State of Life

Liturgy of Reconciliation
- Confession of Sins

Acceptance of Satisfaction
- Penitent's Prayer of Sorrow
- Absolution

The rite begins with the priest inviting the sick person to put his or her trust in God. *Pastoral Care of the Sick* provides three options for this invitation or the priest may use his own words. The *Rite of Penance* only provides

---

101. PCS, 279.

one invitation; however, the priest also has the option to use similar words. The Revelation of State of Life is unique to *Pastoral Care of the Sick*; it does not appear in the *Rite of Penance*. The rubrics suggest that the priest may not know the sick person and this provides an opportunity for him to become somewhat familiar with the sick person's spiritual journey. He might inquire about the time of the person's last confession, any difficulties the person has in leading a Christian life, and "anything that may help the priest to exercise his ministry."[102]

The Liturgy of Reconciliation follows the same pattern as found in the *Rite of Penance*. The penitent may simply make a generic confession, that is, a more general confession of sin without much detail. This option is helpful for the penitent if he or she has trouble remembering or if they are impaired or weakened from their illness. The priest may also help them to make an integral confession by asking questions that help them to review aspects of their spiritual life. The priest gives suitable counsel to the sick person, being sure to be aware of the person's condition of illness and their ability to be attentive. These words of counsel may relate the person's suffering to the suffering of Christ and how the grace he gives us renews the life of the one who repents with a sincere heart.

The priest proposes an act of penance that the sick person accepts as a way to amend their life. The penance should be one that the sick person can complete, either in prayer or in some suitable action that is connected to their sins. The penance may also take the form of meditating on the union of their suffering with Christ.

The priest then asks the penitent to express their sorrow for sin, either in their own words or in an act of contrition that they may already know. The rite provides two other options for the prayer of sorrow. It is very unlikely that the sick person will know these options, so it will be necessary for the priest to have a copy of the rite or a copy of the prayers for the sick person to use. The rite concludes with the prayer of absolution that uses the same words from the *Rite of Penance*.

The concluding blessing is one of the options from the *Rite of Penance*: "The Lord has freed you from sin. / May he bring you safely to his kingdom in heaven. / Glory to him forever. / Amen." Although the words have an appropriate meaning for a healthy penitent, they take on an even deeper

---

102. PCS, 301.

meaning for a person who is sick, and who might also be contemplating the possibility of dying as a result of their illness.

Pastoral Principles

The Parish Community

If one member suffers in the Body of Christ, which is the Church, all the members suffer with that member.[103] Thus, the Church's ministry to the sick and the dying is an essential part of her total ministry to the world. When the Church cares for those who are sick, she serves Christ himself in the suffering members of the Mystical Body of Christ. The communal nature of the revised rites of the *Pastoral Care of the Sick* allow the parish community to reclaim her role and her duty to care for and to accompany those who are sick and dying.

It is fitting "that all the baptized Christians share in this ministry of mutual charity within the Body of Christ by doing all that they can to help the sick return to health, by showing love for the sick, and by celebrating the sacraments with them. Like the other sacraments, these too have a community aspect, which should be brought out as much as possible when they are celebrated."[104]

The celebration of the Sacrament of the Anointing of the Sick is thus a concern of the local Church, the parish, or other faith community. Liturgical celebrations of the sacraments are not private functions but are celebrations belonging to the whole Church. "Whenever rites . . . make provision for communal celebration involving the presence and active participation of the faithful, it is to be stressed that this way of celebrating them is to be preferred."[105] When the local Church gathers to pray over and commend the sick and dying to the Lord she becomes conscious of the ministry she shares with the Lord, and her own participation in the suffering of Christ.

Liturgical services are not private functions, but are celebrations belonging to the Church, which is the "sacrament of unity," namely, the holy people united.

—*Constitution on the Sacred Liturgy*, 26

---

103. See 1 Corinthians 12:26.
104. PCS, 33.
105. CSL, 26.

The Church's ministry to the sick and the dying is an essential part of her total ministry to the world.

Thus, those who are sick or who are dying have a particular ministry to the other members of the Church. In the celebration of the prayers, readings, and gestures of the sacrament, the sick give witness to their promises at Baptism to die and be resurrected to new life in Christ. They give a visible witness that our mortal life is always open to the redemptive grace of God.

The Rites of Anointing and Viaticum and those for the pastoral care of the dying are rooted in the Word of God and are always celebrated with a proclamation of that Word. The proclamation of the Word of God, especially the readings that recall the ministry of Jesus, is a reminder to the whole Church that her spiritual and physical well-being exists within the tender mercy of God.

The prayers, litanies, and various texts of the rites speak of human sickness and its significance in the mystery of salvation. They remind all the faithful of the paradox of our faith: our participation in the Paschal Mystery of Christ through human suffering is imbued with redemptive meaning.

The Church's rituals, especially the Rites of Anointing and Viaticum, are by their very nature forms of pastoral care. The words, music, gestures of touch, and blessings convey an invisible but real sense of empathy and love. This experience can be very moving and comforting for the sick person. Rituals act as the Church's solemn and symbolic proclamation that the reign of God is the ultimate framework of meaning, especially when one's world is shattered by the reality of illness and death.

Not only do Christians need rituals to help those who are suffering, they also need rituals to strengthen and support those who are caring for the suffering.[106] Through ritual celebrations the faith community places a certain interpretation on the chaos and brokenness brought on by some of life's experiences. The symbolic, ritual complex of Word and action permits the community to own both present reality and Christian hope, and to negotiate the often difficult and painful passage between the two.

Pope John Paul II, who surely understood the reality of suffering from personal experience, made a heartfelt plea to people to heed the situation of those who are sick, and who need the compassion of society and of the Church:

> Today I make an urgent plea. Do not neglect your sick and elderly. Do not turn away from the handicapped and the dying. Do not push them to the margins of society. For, if you do, you will fail to understand that they represent an important truth. The sick, the elderly, the handicapped, and the dying teach us that weakness is a creative part of human living, and that suffering can be embraced with no loss of dignity. Without the presence of these people in your midst you might be tempted to think of health, strength, and power as the only important values to be pursued in life. But the wisdom of Christ and the power of Christ are to be seen in the weakness of those who share his sufferings.
>
> Let us keep the sick and the handicapped at the center of our lives. Let us treasure them and recognize with gratitude the debt we owe them. We begin by imagining that we are giving to them; we end by realizing that they have enriched us.[107]

If the words of Pope John Paul II were a universal call to society on behalf of the sick, how much more urgent is the responsibility of the Church to attend to those who are sick and suffering in her midst.

Ministry to the sick and the dying is a fundamental part of the pastoral life of the local Church. There are a number of ways that the parish can exercise this important ministry.

---

106. See Bernard Cooke and Gary Macy, *Christian Symbol and Ritual* (Oxford: Oxford University Press, 2005), 157.

107. Pope John Paul II, Homily at a communal celebration of Anointing the Sick, St. George's Cathedral, Southwark, London, May 28, 1982. Reprinted from Bishops' Committee on the Liturgy, Newsletter XVIII (1982), 22–23.

- A pastoral care team. Depending on the size of the parish, a paid pastoral care coordinator may be necessary to keep track of parish members who are sick. A team of volunteers can be recruited to assist the coordinator with visits to the sick, arrangements for Communion to the sick, working with the liturgy team to prepare communal celebrations of the Sacrament of Anointing, and any other duties that would ensure that those who are sick are not forgotten by the rest of the parish.

- Praying for the sick. Many parishes include the names of the sick in the Universal Prayer. Some parishes have a Book of Intentions in which family members can write the names of the sick and a general intention is spoken during the Universal Prayer for "those whose names are in our book of intentions."

- Communal celebrations. Parishes can schedule and publicize communal celebrations of the Sacraments of Anointing and Viaticum so that all parishioners can gather in prayerful support of the sick. These celebrations should include the various liturgical ministries, such as hospitality, music, readers, Communion assistants, servers, and the liturgical environment.

A team of volunteers may be trained to assist pastoral care ministers with visits to the sick.

The sick and the handicapped should be at the center of our lives, treasured, and recognized with gratitude.

- Special days in the liturgical calendar. The Church's sanctoral cycle (the commemorations of the saints) provides an opportunity for the parish to call attention to those who are sick: for example, February 11, the Feast of Our Lady of Lourdes and the World Day of the sick; the Feast of St. Vincent de Paul; and other feast days that commemorate the women and men who founded religious communities that had a special ministry to the sick. The homily on these days could reference the presence of the sick in the parish, noting their witness to those who are well, and calling attention to the how all the faithful share in the suffering of Christ. One or more of these days could be an occasion for a communal celebration of the sacrament of anointing the sick.

- Some parishes have initiated the practice of dismissing pastoral care ministers after the Communion Rite at Sunday Masses. The priest says these or similar words:

We ask God's blessing on you and this good ministry that you have taken up on our behalf. We send you out to those who are our brothers and sisters but who were unable to join us today. We send you with the gift of our love and the promise of our prayers for them, and with the Body of Christ to strengthen them.

- Pastoral care ministers can help those they visit stay connected to the parish by taking the parish bulletin to them, as well as blessed palms on Palm Sunday, any notices of events in the parish, handouts that the parish makes available during Advent and Lent, and any material that would communicate to the sick that even in their absence they are remembered.

- Cards and letters. One parish has a "cards and letters" group who send get-well cards to those who are sick, as well as birthday cards to those who live in retirement residences and long term care homes. The cards bring a little cheer to the recipients and let them know that others are thinking of them.

- Special visitors. Visiting the sick is one of the traditional works of mercy. Some parishes organize group visits to nursing homes by the Confirmation candidates. Of course good planning is necessary, but reports have been very positive and often some of the young people have asked to be part of the pastoral care ministry. Special visits by the music ministry is another popular and caring practice, especially prior to Christmas.

- Pastoral care ministers take up their ministry on behalf of the whole parish, but others could be encouraged to join this ministry or to offer a "ministry of accompaniment" from time to time. This might include accompanying the priest or pastoral visitor to residences and hospitals where there are a number of sick persons. In addition to the few moments that elapse for the actual rite, whether for communion or an anointing by a priest, a few moments can be spent simply visiting with the person who is sick. Sharing stories about the life of the parish, reading Scripture passages or passages from their favorite book, and assisting them to take a walk, if they are able, are some ways to accompany them, as a good shepherd might for those who need a gentle touch in life.

- Respite care. One of the positive trends in health care is known as palliative care. This is described by Pope Francis as "an expression of the properly human attitude of taking care of one another, especially those who suffer. It bears witness that the human person is always precious, even if marked by age and sickness."[108] Many communities have established palliative care sites, some are free standing and others are located within a hospital. In many situations those in palliative care actually reside in their

---

108. Pope Francis, Address to the Pontifical Academy of Life, March 2015.

own home and palliative care staff assist family members in providing the necessary care, often twenty-four hours a day. Parishes could initiate a home visit team that would allow family members some "respite" time. These pastoral care ministers would be available to do various errands or to stay with the sick person while the family members themselves take care of other obligations, like grocery shopping.

Multicultural Considerations and Adaptations in the Rite

One of the radical and refreshing principles that the *Constitution on the Sacred Liturgy* introduced as a reason for the renewal of the liturgy and the subsequent revisions of ritual books was the importance of culture.[109] It is clear that the Council understood the importance of culture in fostering and enriching the faith of peoples within the universal Church. Culture is intertwined with the various expressions and conventions of any faith tradition. The sacramental life of the Catholic Church is integral to faith and thus is affected and even shaped by culture. Cultural practices, including language, that are "in keeping with the true and authentic spirit of the liturgy"[110] can and should be admitted into the celebration of the liturgy. In this regard, competent ecclesiastical authority may "carefully and prudently weigh what elements from the traditions and culture of individual peoples may be appropriately admitted into divine worship."[111] Such liturgical adaptations, inclusions, or retentions may take several forms. Inculturation refers to substantial change in the liturgy for a certain nation or region. Adaptation is also a substantial change to the Roman Rite, known as the typical edition, and comes under the jurisdiction of the episcopal conference of a particular country or region. Accommodation within the rite is more local in that it is initiated by the minister of the rite and is based on concrete pastoral circumstances.[112]

The "General Introduction" to *Pastoral Care of the Sick* states that "the number of anointings may be increased and the place of anointing changed" depending on the "culture and traditions of different peoples."[113] The notes then add that "directives on this should be included in the preparation of

---

109. See CSL, 37–40.

110. CSL, 37.

111. CSL, 40.

112. For a commentary on these three distinctions see Rev. Michael Driscoll, *General Introduction to "The Constitution on the Scared Liturgy,"* Liturgy Documents, vol. 1, 5th ed., xv.

113. PCS, 24.

particular rituals."[114] The rubrics within the Rite of Anointing reference this allowance, giving the example of anointing the place of pain or injury as an example of a cultural influence.[115]

However, the principle alluding to culture as a determining factor for adaptations of the rite seems to be a general principle, as there aren't any specific cultural adaptations listed, apart from noting the "place of pain or injury" as a place for an anointing. Other adaptations related to culture may be possible and legitimate.[116] However, the current ritual makes no mention of such examples. The option for shortening the rite, or changing the texts or choosing different readings in the respective rites is based on the condition of the sick person and not culture. This differs from the *Order for Celebrating Matrimony*, as an example, which includes the Blessing and Giving of the *Arras* and the Blessing and Placing of the *Lazo* or the Veil in the celebration. These two blessings and gestures are cultural in origin and do not require any authorization on the part of the liturgical minister.

The implications for the Anointing of the Sick are less obvious, and as noted, not described within the rite itself. It seems that the onus is on the liturgical minister to discover what, if any, cultural custom might be respected in the rite of anointing and care of the dying. As long as the accommodations are in "keeping with the true and authentic spirit of the liturgy" it falls under the condition set by the *Constitution*. The *Constitution* states the same principle by noting that these added elements must not be "bound up with superstition or error."[117]

What cultural accommodations might be permitted? One thinks of hymns that are familiar to the sick person and his or her family and that can be sung in their native language. Although there is more to culture than language, language is a significant vehicle of culture and can be a source of healing. Another cultural expression is in the gesture of touch, being able to embrace the person who is sick or is dying. This ministry of comfort may also include a preparation ritual of the body by family members. This is a laudable act that, in its own way, is countercultural to the often clinical

---

114. PCS, 24.

115. PCS, 24.

116. *Pastoral Care of the Sick* allows for the Conferences of Bishops to decide on adaptations based on the traditions and culture of individual peoples, which need to be submitted to the Apostolic See for approval; see the "General Introduction," 38.

117. CSL, 37.

approach by medical staff or funeral directors who tend to put an emphasis on efficiency and urgency.

Another cultural accommodation is the inclusion of a religious image that has a certain spiritual meaning for the sick or the dying person. Such examples include a crucifix, an image of the Blessed Mother, for example Our Lady of Guadalupe, a rosary or another religious object that carries both meaning and comfort for the person.

Pastoral Care of the Sick also allows the individual pastoral minister to make certain adaptations in the celebration of the various rites based on a number of circumstances. Among those is the condition of the sick person and their ability to be attentive to, or to participate in the rite; the suitability of the location for the celebration of the rite in its full form; and the probable imminence of death when celebrating rites for the dying (in this case a shorter form of the rite is available). The pastoral minister may also adapt the rite depending on the wishes of the sick person; for example, whether or not they desire to confess during the rite of anointing.[118] Although not explicitly an adaption, the rite provides an entire section[119] from which the minister can choose various texts that would be more suited to the actual pastoral situation. The minister also has some freedom in choosing his or her reflection or instruction during the rite so that their words will address the more specific condition of the sick or the dying.

Pastoral ministers should remember that appropriate accommodations to the liturgical rites is never to placate or humor the sick or dying, or their family, not even for the sake of the liturgical act, but for the spiritual nourishment offered to the members of Christ's Body. The gestures, objects, words, and rhythm of the Church's rituals can manifest the presence of God in the lives of those who have special need of the assurance of divine compassion.

---

118. See PCS, 40–41.
119. See PCS, Part III: Readings, Responses, and Verses from Sacred Scripture.

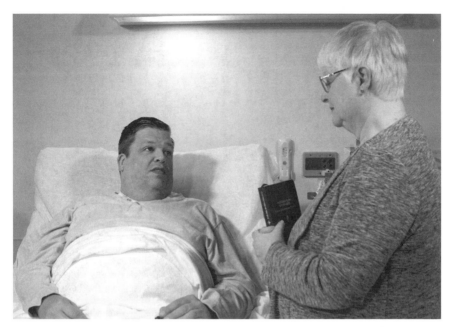

The minister may adapt his or her reflection to the specific conditions of the sick person.

Interacting with Families

The pastoral exercise of interacting and connecting with families is a full time ministry for pastors and lay pastoral ministers. This ministry is exacerbated in our time by a number of factors: the decline in the numbers of ordained clergy; the clustering of parishes and the consequent size of parish membership; the demographic of an aging population, both among clergy and members of the faithful; the broad range of living situations for those who are sick or dying. This latter issue is a good thing as the sick and dying have more suitable options for their care. At the same time it presents the pastoral minister with several locations to cover in their ministry. A recent development in health care institutions has been the issue of confidentiality. The religion of residents is no longer readily available to pastoral visitors and it can be difficult to track down the members of a particular faith community without a specific referral from a family member.

These factors notwithstanding, pastoral ministers are dedicated to their ministry and do everything they can to offer compassion and prayerful support to those who are sick and dying. Anyone who has ever worked in pastoral care ministry, whether on a parish team or as part of a pastoral ministry team in an institutional setting, knows that when a person is ill or is in danger

Interacting with families is a full time ministry for pastors and lay pastoral ministers.

of dying, other schedules and agendas are put on hold in order to care for the person and their immediate families.

The range of emotions that accompanies an illness or the prospect of dying is varied and extensive. This is true both for the person and for their respective families and friends. Pastoral care ministers need an abundance of patience, calm, and confidence. Equally important is being able to resist the temptation to be the rescuer, that is, the person who takes over the reality of another's pain and suffering. Staying connected is important, but a comforting presence does not include being the therapist, the medical staff person or the life counsellor. The pastoral minister is the spiritual presence, a role that is as important, if not more so, than any other.

Parishes usually develop various ways to keep connected with those who are ill or dying. The most common practice is receiving the information from a spouse or other family member. Keeping track of the person's situation requires lots of time calling, visiting, plus untold hours to do follow up. Good communication between the members of the pastoral care team is essential.

Every situation will have its own characteristics: if the person who is sick or dying is a child; if they are a victim of an accident, a crime, or unexpected health crisis; if they are estranged from their spouse and or family members; if they are living at a considerable distance from other family members. All these factors affect the ways that a pastoral care minister interacts with the sick or dying person. The reality of sickness and the real possibility of dying are never separated from the larger experience of life.

> The family and friends of the sick and those who take care of them in any way have a special share in this ministry of comfort.
>
> —*Pastoral Care of the Sick*, 34

The pastoral care minister must never "take sides" if there is some dispute about care or arrangements. They should avoid making demands and pronouncing ultimatums related to Church policies until there is an environment of calm; and then gentleness, understanding, and compassion are always a better option. It may be helpful to ask, "How would I like to be treated if this was my family member?" The pastoral care minister is always a sign of and the bearer of the compassion of Christ. Maybe the best approach is found in that popular question, "What would Jesus do?"

Pastoral Care in Difficult Situations

"A health care crisis presents unique issues of spiritual and moral meaning."[120] No matter how strong one thinks their faith is, or how composed they are in most of life's situations, a diagnosis of serious illness for oneself or a loved one can become a stressful and uncertain journey with no map or GPS as a guide.[121]

Most every situation involving illness and dying can be difficult for those who are involved, including the pastoral care minister. Often difficult decisions need to be made about treatments, the possibility of a move to an unfamiliar environment, or the availability of the necessary resources, such as finances and supportive care by family members. Although advances in modern health care often lead, happily, to recovery, some situations can be more difficult than others. For example, the death of a child, especially an infant; the death of a victim of a crime; an illness that is diagnosed as terminal; the decision to discontinue the means of life support; the unexpected death of a parent of young children; a sudden illness that results in paralysis or serious brain damage.

---

120. Nuala Kenny, SC, OC, MD, FRCP, *Rediscovering the Art of Dying, How Jesus' Experience and our Stories Reveal a New Vision of Compassionate Care* (Toronto, ON: Novalis, 2018), 21.

121. See Kenny, 21.

The pastoral minister should always be the bearer of Christ.

In all these, and many other situations, the pastoral care minister needs to "dig deep" into their spiritual well to offer support and consolation to immediate family members, and often to others such as close friends and colleagues.

The pastoral care minister is the spiritual presence. However, when he or she encounters an extraordinarily difficult situation, a formal rite or even a less formal moment of prayer may not be the first thing one should offer. That is not to say that prayer should be postponed, let alone omitted, but perhaps there needs to be time for everyone to collect their thoughts, soothe their emotions, and regain some composure. Often those who are closest to the situation will be the ones who will give permission for the pastoral care minister to engage others in prayer.

The minister should discern what, if any, adaptations need to be made to the rite in order to be sensitive to the situation. Also, an invitation to participate should be extended to all who are present; that includes those who may not be Catholic and any health care staff. The time for "leave taking" may be difficult when family members need to leave the room or the hospital in order to make any arrangements in the case of a death. The pastoral care minister should be as helpful as possible at that time, and offer to assist with the necessary arrangements, without necessarily taking charge. The minister should assure the persons affected by the illness or death that they will be available for any assistance needed in the ensuing days. It would be important to exchange contact information and to follow up with one or more of the family members beyond those days and into the foreseeable future. If the situation involves a death, and the parish has a grief counsel or a ministry for grieving persons, then let people know that they can count on those persons for ongoing support.

In addition to ministering to the adults who are connected to this difficult situation, the pastoral minister may be called on to provide comfort for young children. This may entail a brief conversation or a more lengthy discussion at a later time. The minister's best approach is honesty and simplicity. Children are usually not interested in theological explanations and it is good practice to answer simply and offer only as much information as asked for. If children are present when the prayers are said they can be asked to contribute their own prayer. In these difficult situations the pastoral minister learns that the ministry of presence is most often the most needed and the most appreciated.

The Liturgical Year and Pastoral Care

Advent

One of the traditional themes of Advent is waiting. Those who celebrate the Sacrament of the Anointing of the Sick are often very conscious of what it means to wait. It may be that they are waiting for surgery, test results, relief from pain, or assurance that they will regain a sense of wellness once again. It is during those times that they can benefit from the Sacrament of Anointing, not only spiritually but emotionally. Indeed, many have said that the prayers and gestures of the rite have given them a sense that their spirits have been renewed and their body improved.

Pastoral Care of the Sick offers many options for readings from Scripture. During Advent priests and pastoral care ministers could also choose readings from the Sundays and weekdays of Advent. Here are some suggestions:

- First Week of Advent: the psalm refrain for Sunday; the First Reading for Wednesday; the psalm for Friday; or the psalm for Saturday.

- Second Week of Advent: the Second Reading for Sunday; the psalms for Wednesday, Thursday, or Saturday.

- Third Week of Advent: the First Reading for Sunday; the psalms for Sunday, Monday, or Tuesday.

- Fourth Week of Advent: the psalm for December 19; the Gospel for December 21, the psalms for December 23, or December 24.

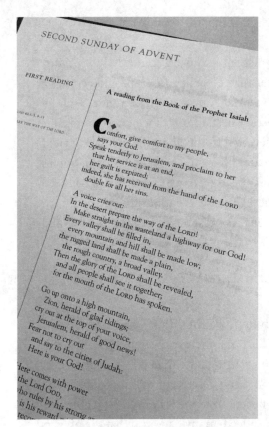

SECOND SUNDAY OF ADVENT

FIRST READING

A reading from the Book of the Prophet Isaiah

Comfort, give comfort to my people,
says your God.
Speak tenderly to Jerusalem, and proclaim to her
that her service is at an end,
her guilt is expiated;
indeed, she has received from the hand of the LORD
double for all her sins.

A voice cries out:
In the desert prepare the way of the LORD!
Make straight in the wasteland a highway for our God!
Every valley shall be filled in,
every mountain and hill shall be made low;
the rugged land shall be made a plain,
the rough country, a broad valley.
Then the glory of the LORD shall be revealed,
and all people shall see it together;
for the mouth of the LORD has spoken.

Go up onto a high mountain,
Zion, herald of glad tidings;
cry out at the top of your voice,
Jerusalem, herald of good news!
Fear not to cry out
and say to the cities of Judah:
Here is your God!

Here comes with power
the Lord GOD,
who rules by his strong a..
is his reward ..
rec...

There are many options for selecting Scripture readings. Let the Sunday Lectionary be your guide.

The pastoral intent of the Sacrament of the Anointing of the Sick, with the Scripture readings, prayers, gestures, and presence of others echoes the command of the Lord to the prophet Isaiah: "Comfort, give comfort to my people, / says your God."[122]

Christmas Time

Much of the energy associated with Christmas, both in pastoral ministry and in family life, is found in the closing days of Advent and on the eve of the Solemnity of the Nativity of the Lord. The many activities of parish life are all wonderful celebrations that emphasize the nature of community and help to express the bonds of relationship within the parish and give it a feeling of joy and gratitude as the people of the Lord.

Many parishes engage in outreach projects by placing gift tags on a giving tree that encourage parishioners to purchase gifts that are distributed to families in the larger community. The intention is to ensure that no one be left out at Christmas.

Among those who often feel "left out" at Christmas are people who are homebound or hospitalized because of their health. There are also those for whom Christmas brings back memories of sadness related to a death of a loved one, either during the past year or in prior years.

The feelings of loss and loneliness can be overwhelming. Pastoral Care ministers need to be especially attentive to those who find themselves in such situations. The Sacrament of the Anointing of the Sick can bring great comfort to people whose health has not allowed them to join in the festivities of their parish family or to be with their own family members.

---

122. Isaiah 40:1.

However, since other family members may be visiting from elsewhere during these days it is a wonderful opportunity to bring them together for a celebration of the sacrament with the person who is ill. The pastor and pastoral care visitors can take reminders of the parish to the sick person, for example the Christmas bulletin or a small plant to leave in the person's room. Some parishioners could be invited to pen notes or sign Christmas cards as a reminder that the person is still present in the thoughts and prayers of the parishioners.

Sometimes pastoral care visitors, including clergy, find it difficult to express the sense of joy that pervades this time of year when they are confronted with someone who is not feeling the same emotions. A possible conversation topic can be sharing stories and memories, both happy ones and those that are not as uplifting, about family traditions related to Christmas. This allows an opportunity for the sick person to feel included in the world around them, even when they are not as engaged as they once were.

There are several Scripture readings from this time that offer suitable reflections for the celebration of anointing. Suggestions include the psalm from the Feast of St. Stephen, martyr (December 27); the First Reading from the Feast of St. John the Evangelist (December 27); the Second Reading (Year A) and the psalm (Year C) for the Feast of the Holy Family.

Since the Solemnity of Mary, the Holy Mother of God, (New Year's Day) falls in this period of time, a communal celebration of the Anointing of the Sick could be scheduled in the first few days of the New Year. Those who are ill might see a spiritual connection between the comforting grace of the sacrament and their own desire to begin the year under the protection of Mary who brought such solace to her son in his suffering.

Ordinary Time during the Winter

In Year B there are three successive healing stories from Mark on the Fourth, Fifth, and Sixth Sundays. These Scripture texts provide the homilist with good sources for preaching about the remarkable intervention of God through the power of the Spirit in human affairs, especially in the times when suffering and brokenness enter our lives. The encounters of Jesus with those he heals are moments of compassion and mercy.

Since the Anointing of the Sick, like all the sacraments, is more fully expressed when it is a communal celebration, the parish should consider arranging for such a celebration on one of these Sundays. Perhaps the

The Blessing of the Throats may be included in the liturgy of the Anointing of the Sick.

obvious choice of the three Sundays would be the Sunday closest to February 11, the optional memorial of Our Lady of Lourdes and the World Day of the Sick.

The Anointing of the Sick could take place during the Sunday liturgies using the shorter form of the rite. Such a celebration requires a good deal of preparation including announcements well ahead of time so people can make arrangements to be present. Extra ministers of hospitality will be needed for those who require assistance. Transportation from health care residences will need to be provided. Although a special liturgy could be scheduled apart from the regular Sunday Masses, there is a profound witness given to the whole parish when the sacrament is celebrated with the community. The pastoral notes for the rite speak of the witness that those who are sick give to others; a witness that reflects the redemptive grace that flows to all of us from Christ's own suffering.

Two other days during this season can be opportunities to highlight the place of this sacrament in the life of the parish. On the Feast of the Presentation of the Lord (February 2) it is customary to bless and distribute candles. The Gospel passage from Luke tells the moving story of Jesus' parents meeting Simeon and Anna in the Temple. The Canticle of Simeon is a beautiful prayer for those who are experiencing great sickness, and could bring some comfort to those whose illness is terminal.

Pastoral ministers should bring prayer booklets and worship aids to those they minister.

Pastoral care visitors could take one of the blessed candles to give to those they visit as a reminder that the whole parish continues to keep them in prayer. On February 3, the Church celebrates the optional Memorial of St. Blaise. The custom of blessing throats on this day is kept in many parishes and could be part of a liturgy of Anointing of the Sick. Pastoral care ministers may also bless the throats of those whom they visit on this day; the prayer of blessing is found in the *Book of Blessings* (chapter 51).

Lent and Holy Week

The themes of reconciliation and healing are the spiritual touchstones for the season of Lent. The Anointing of the Sick can appropriately be included in the liturgical practices of the parish. There are many Scripture passages in the Lectionary options for Lent that would be suitable selections for either a communal celebration of Anointing or for the celebration with an individual.

The parish might consider scheduling a communal Anointing of the Sick on the Monday of Holy Week. The Scripture readings for this weekday are especially suited for a celebration of the sacrament. An invitation should be extended to the whole parish to participate in this liturgy. St. Paul reminds us that if any members of the Body of Christ, the Church, suffer, then all members suffer with them.[123] When the Church gathers to pray for and

---

123. See 1 Corinthians 12:26.

support those who are ill it fulfills its identity as Christ's body and exercises its ministry of compassion.

During the season of Lent parishes often schedule special celebrations like the Stations of the Cross, Lenten missions, or evenings of reflection. It may be possible for those who are homebound to access these on the parish website, or through live-streaming programs. Pastoral care visitors should remember to take any printed material, like prayer booklets, to those they visit.

Often those who are ill feel a certain isolation from the parish community; every effort should be made to bridge that sense of separation that they experience.

A simple gesture is for the pastoral care visitors to take blessed ashes at the beginning of Lent to those they visit. The mark of ashes connects them to the Lenten journey of the whole Church. Also, by taking blessed palms to them, they are reminded of their membership within the community of believers as they enter Holy Week. This also allows them to have a connection with the sufferings of Christ himself in a way that can be deeply moving and spiritually renewing.

Sacred Paschal Triduum

Although there are some restrictions on the celebration of ritual Masses during the Sacred Triduum, for example weddings and funerals, the Anointing of the Sick can be celebrated at any time. Ordinarily a communal Anointing of the Sick would not be scheduled during the Sacred Paschal Triduum. Holy Communion may be taken to those who are sick at any time during the Sacred Triduum. The exception is on Holy Saturday when communion can only be given if the person is dying. In that case the Rite for Viaticum is celebrated.[124]

At some point during Holy Week, the oils to be used for sacramental rites in the parish are blessed by the bishop during the Chrism Mass celebrated at the cathedral church of the diocese. Traditionally this liturgy is celebrated on Holy Thursday (although some dioceses schedule it on another day). Many parishes choose to receive the blessed oils in a brief rite just prior to the celebration of the Liturgy of the Lord's Supper on Thursday evening. In this ritual each of the blessed oils is presented, a prayer of thanksgiving is said and the vessels of oil are placed in the ambry. One or more ministers of

---

124. See Chapter 5, Celebration of Viaticum, Pastoral Care of the Sick, Rites of Anointing and Viaticum.

pastoral care could present the oil of the sick. Again, this brief ritual serves to connect the entire parish with the many individuals whose sacramental journey is not always as visible within the congregation. It also reminds the parish of its own ministry toward those who are sick.

It is most fitting that Communion be taken to those who are unable to join the assembly for the liturgies of the Sacred Triduum. Perhaps the ideal time to do this is after the Liturgy of the Lord's Supper on Holy Thursday. Sending forth the pastoral ministers after this liturgy makes a visible statement on how the Body of Christ, the Church, extends beyond the gathered assembly and embraces those whose absence is acknowledged in the prayer of the community.

However, this might pose a practical concern in that the liturgy, which is normally scheduled in the evening, may not be concluded until quite late. This might not be the best time to be visiting the homes or health care residences of those who are sick. The other option is after the Communion Rite on the afternoon of Good Friday.

It is appropriate for the pastoral care minister to offer a few words of reflection on the passion of Christ, including some reference to how the parish is celebrating the Sacred Triduum.

Easter Time

Pastoral Care of the Sick is firmly rooted in the theology of the Paschal Mystery. As the Church continues to celebrate the life, death, and Resurrection of Christ during Easter Time, she does so with thanksgiving for the redemptive grace of Christ's sacrifice and for the outpouring of a new life of freedom and mercy through his Resurrection.

In the Gospel readings for Easter Time we encounter the remarkable words and gestures of Jesus as he assures us of the love of the Father. His greeting of peace to the disciples, found in the Gospel texts for the

Second Sunday is passed on to us in the words and gestures of the Eucharistic liturgy. No matter what our situation in life we yearn for the peace that only the Lord can give.

The image of Jesus as the Good Shepherd (Fourth Sunday, Year A, B, C) brings great comfort to us whenever we encounter brokenness in our lives. On the Fifth Sunday, Year A, we read the words, "do not let your hearts be troubled." The Gospel message for us in the Gospel accounts of the Sixth Sunday is simply this, "As the Father loves me, so I also love you."

Easter Time affirms the ministry of the Church as the ministry of the Risen Christ at work in the world. The pastoral notes from the *Pastoral Care of Sick* state that this ministry is the common responsibility of all Christians. Parishes are encouraged to explore various ways of reaching out to those who are sick.

Ordinary Time during the Summer and Fall

When we think of the liturgical life of the Church, there is nothing really "ordinary" about how the community of faith celebrates the unfolding of the Paschal Mystery in its midst. During these weeks of the liturgical calendar the Sacrament of the Anointing of the Sick is celebrated against the backdrop of the Scriptures, especially the Gospel accounts of Jesus' healing ministry.

The experiences of suffering, illness, and death have no time or season in the scope of human affairs. The encounters of Jesus with those who sought his words of comfort and his healing touch often occurred in the most ordinary circumstances in people's lives. The Sacrament of the Anointing of the Sick is intended to bring that same ministry to people today.

As the Church continues to explore the grace and the demands of the mission of the Risen Lord, his healing ministry is taken up in every time and place by men and women who seek to embody his compassion and grace.

If the parish has not scheduled opportunities for the pastoral care ministers to gather for some form of renewal in their ministry this would be an ideal time to do that. A number of topics could be addressed in such a session; for example, the history of the Rite of Anointing, the theology of suffering, and the ministry of the Church as the ministry of Christ. The prayers and Scripture readings found in the various rites offer rich spiritual nourishment for such gatherings. Those who take up this ministry need to nourish their own spiritual well-being on a regular basis.

Opportunities for Evangelization

The word *evangelization* has its roots in the Greek word *evangelion* and the Latin word *evangelium*. *Evangelization* may be understood as "the process of proclaiming the good news (the Gospel) and enabling the good news to be accepted readily by those people disposed by grace to receive it."[125]

The term *evangelization* is a more recent addition to the theological literature of the Roman Catholic Church, having been included in several of the documents of the Second Vatican Council. In his encyclical letter of 1975 *Evangelii nuntiandi,* Pope Paul VI spoke of evangelization as a process of conversion both individually and culturally. The more traditional understanding of evangelization as the work of missionaries converting unbelievers to Christianity has thus been expanded to mean an inward dimension of "renewal and re-conversion"[126] for believers themselves. Thus, it could be said that evangelization includes all those activities that encourage, support, and enrich the renewal of the Christian community in its commitment to spreading and acting upon the Gospel of Jesus Christ.

Evangelization is not catechesis or an academic program, although at some point shared information can be very helpful for those returning to a practice of faith. Evangelization is an awakening or the reawakening of the thirst for the way and the Word of the Lord. Evangelization thrives in an atmosphere of hospitality and with the assurances of God's mercy.

The responsibility of evangelization belongs to the whole Church. As Pope Paul VI noted, "Evangelizing is in fact the grace and vocation proper to the Church, her deepest identity. She exists in order to evangelize, that is to say, in order to preach and teach, to be the channel of the gift of grace, to reconcile sinners with God, and to perpetuate Christ's sacrifice in the Mass, which is the memorial of His death and glorious resurrection."[127] The mission of the Church is clearly set forth by Christ himself when he "co-missions" the disciples, "Go into the whole world and proclaim the gospel to every creature."[128] It can be said that evangelization is the central mission of the Church.

Among the many works of the Church in her mission of evangelization, the liturgical celebrations of the sacraments are most laudable. Through the

---

125. Frank DeSiano, CSJ, *The New Dictionary of Sacramental Worship*, ed. Peter Fink, SJ (Collegeville, MN: Liturgical Press, 1990), 464.

126. DeSiano, 464.

127. *Evangelii nuntiandi*, 14.

128. Mark 16:15.

proclamation of the Good News of Jesus Christ each of the sacraments calls participants to their own inward renewal. At the same time, by virtue of their public and communal nature, the sacraments give witness to Jesus Christ who invites everyone to believe in the Good News of salvation. The sacramental rites of the Church are acts of evangelization.

In the Sacrament of Anointing of the Sick and in her ministry to the dying, the Church carries out her ministry by visible acts of compassion and consolation. The proclamation of the Word of God, even in a short passage that is shared during the various rites, is an occasion of evangelization. When the Word of God is proclaimed it not only announces the tender concern of Christ the Good Shepherd for those who are ill and dying, it also brings comfort to those who accompany the sick and the dying.

> Evangelizing means bringing the Good News of Jesus into all the strata of humanity, and through its influence transforming humanity from within and making it new.
>
> —*Evangelii nuntiandi*, 18

The Sacrament of Anointing recalls the many acts of healing in Jesus' own ministry. Just as those encounters were signs of the reign of God, so too is the reign of God made present in the sacramental practice of the Church today. In the rites of anointing there is a mutual experience of evangelization. The recipients of the sacrament are a beautiful sign of the reciprocity of this sacrament. On the one hand, the priest and community care for the sick; and on the other, the sick contribute through their suffering to the faith and salvation of the community and the world.[129]

When the Rites of Anointing are celebrated in a communal setting, they are a powerful and public expression of the evangelizing ministry of the Church. Frequently these communal celebrations become invitations to participants to renew or to make more mature their life of faith, especially if they have been struggling in their faith, or have been absent from the sacramental life of the Church.

In the work of evangelizing the Church does not act on her own but is prompted by the Holy Spirit. The evangelizing efforts of the Church build on the grace of Baptism, that first moment when the Word of God was celebrated and the mandate to live out the teachings of Christ was imparted.

---

129. See Randy Stice, *Sacraments of Healing: A Rite-Based Approach* (Chicago: Liturgy Training Publications, 2015), 133.

Baptized into Christ the faithful are sent forth in the power of the Holy Spirit to evangelize: to seek out the lost, the suffering, the poor, the marginalized, the broken, and the forgotten ones. In these ways they make present the healing ministry of Jesus himself and bring the life-changing message of God's love to

> The joy of the gospel fills the hearts and lives of all who encounter Jesus. Those who accept his offer of salvation are set free from sin, sorrow, inner emptiness and loneliness.
>
> —*Evangelii gaudium*, 1

those who are burdened by illness and pain. The pastoral notes for the Rites of Anointing emphasize this communal mandate that belongs to the whole Church as a sharing in the Christ's healing ministry. "It is thus especially fitting that all baptized Christians share in this ministry of mutual charity within the Body of Christ by doing all they can to help the sick return to health, by showing love for the sick, and by celebrating the sacraments with them. Like the other sacraments, these too have a community aspect, which should be brought out as much as possible when they are celebrated."[130]

Pastoral Suggestions for Evangelization

> An evangelizing community . . . has an endless desire to show mercy, the fruit of its own experience of the Father's infinite mercy. . . . An evangelizing community gets involved by word and deed in people's lives; it bridges distances, it is willing to abase itself if necessary and it embraces human life, touching the suffering flesh of Christ in others. . . . An evangelizing community is also supportive, standing by people at every step of the way, no matter how difficult or lengthy this may prove to be.[131]

The Resurrection of Jesus Christ, and his mandate to his first disciples (Matthew 9:35) challenges every faith community "to move from words to action and to develop environments of support and care that provide tangible experiences of God's mercy and that lessen the suffering of the sick, the chronically ill, frail and dependent elderly, the dying and the bereaved."[132] The following are offered for those who prepare and preside at celebrations of anointing and those who engage in the pastoral care of the dying.

---

130. PCS, 33.
131. *Evangelii gaudium*, 24.
132. Kenny, 162.

Always ensure that hospitality is offered at communal celebrations.

- Prepare notices for the communal celebrations of the Anointing of the Sick, whether they are during a regularly scheduled Mass or at another time when the whole community would be able to participate. These notices should be posted well in advance in the parish bulletin, on the parish website or social media page as well as in the entrance way of the church, the school, the parish ministry center—any place where members of the parish as well as visitors will notice. Even outdoor signage can be a good way to let people know that there is an upcoming celebration of the Sacrament of the Anointing of the Sick.

- For communal celebrations, ensure that hospitality is provided. Gestures of hospitality can help folks be disposed to enter into the liturgy and made to feel that they belong among the people of God. This is especially true for those who may not have been to church for a long time, or for those who might be visitors from a neighboring parish. Greeters and hospitality ministers should be ready to assist people with navigating the seating arrangement, locating restrooms, and letting them know how long the liturgy might take.

- Provide a worship aid so that people can participate! Do not assume that those participating will know or be familiar with the prayers and responses. If only the liturgical ministers know how the rite unfolds it sends a message to the assembly that their participation is not that important. The worship aid should include the order of service, music (be sure to secure proper copyright permission) or at least the hymn numbers from the hymnal, as well as the responses and acclamations. If possible, include Scripture readings and the prayers of blessing so participants can take the worship aid home with them. Often those who are ill find it difficult to concentrate even on the prayers with which they are familiar. A different set of prayers or Scripture readings can help them to pray on their own.

- Liturgy teams that prepare communal celebrations of Anointing need to keep in mind the conditions of the sick person when choosing the Scripture readings, the prayers, and the intercessions. The readings and the homily "should help those present to reach a deeper understanding of the mystery of human suffering in relation to the paschal mystery of Christ."[133]

- The homily, or a reflection on the Scripture texts, can offer the pastoral minister an opportunity to evangelize; that is, to explore the reality of human suffering within the context of God's love and the Church's mission to offer hope, even in the midst of human brokenness. Unless there are serious reasons for doing so, the homily should not be omitted. It is a primary vehicle for evangelization, or reevangelization of the faithful who constantly struggle with the questions, and even doubts about the reason for suffering in the world. The challenge for the Church and her rites for the sick is first to take a stand on human suffering, to acknowledge it as something to be struggled against, and then to imbue it with meaning.[134] The entire Rite of

Any celebration with the sick within or outside Mass, at home, in church, or in an institution, may include the singing of hymns.

---

133. PCS, 100.

134. See Lizette Larson-Miller, *The Sacrament of Anointing of the Sick* (Collegeville, MN: Liturgical Press, 2005), 111.

Anointing, as well as those rites associated with pastoral care of the dying, is a profound and public expression of the Church's belief that suffering has meaning and that God has not abandoned the sick.

- Those involved with music ministry have a wonderful opportunity to proclaim the Good News by the choice of music selections for celebrations of Anointing. Most contemporary hymnals have an index that arranges chants and hymns according to themes, ritual celebrations, and liturgical seasons. Many hymn texts are based on Scripture passages. The challenge for the music leader will be which hymns to choose from the many which are available. In selecting suitable hymns, preference should be given to those that are familiar to the congregation. If there are a large number to be anointed, psalm chants can be interspersed with periods of silence during the actual Rite of Anointing.

- The parish communal celebrations offer an opportunity to promote other events in the parish that might be of interest to those who are seeking further support and encouragement in their spiritual journey. If the parish has Scripture study groups, adult faith formation opportunities, gatherings for the Liturgy of the Hours, special evenings such as a holy hour from time to time, and so on, providing an informative pamphlet about these events is a simple act of evangelization. These pamphlets can be given out after the celebration concludes.

- From time to time the Church could, and should respond to events in society that affect members of the community beyond those who are members of the parish, or who are participants in other faith traditions. A contemporary understanding of evangelization regards it as more than the historical missionary efforts to unbelievers who lived in foreign lands. Today the Church can reach out to local communities in ways that can help others to find a spiritual resource in times of unrest. When violence, disasters, and events that cause anxiety and hurt happen in the world around us, there is a commonly felt need for healing. Recall the many ecumenical prayer services that took place in the aftermath of the tragedy of September 11, 2001.

- The local parish community can host a nonsacramental healing service. *Pastoral Care of the Sick* does not offer an order of service for this public need. However, a parish liturgy team could prepare a liturgy that would address this concern. By drawing on the readings and prayers in the rite

110

and developing other elements such as litanies and intercessions, an appropriate celebration could be prepared. Such a liturgy acknowledges the need for healing affecting the broader community in its search for meaning and hope. In this way, the local Church acknowledges her mission as an evangelizing people and recognizes that the work of the Holy Spirit encompasses all peoples in the world around us.

It is true to say that all the sacraments of the Church are sacraments of God's mercy. In Jesus Christ, the Word became flesh; so the word of the Church also assumes concrete shape in the sacraments. Each sacrament in its own way celebrates the unity and love of Jesus Christ which binds us to the deepest unity in and with Jesus Christ, and with one another, and through which we are sent into the world in the service of love and mercy.[135] This is the central focus and understanding of evangelization.

Human Suffering, Christian Hope

"Suffering and illness have always been among the greatest problems that trouble the human spirit."[136] These opening words of the "General Introduction" to *Pastoral Care of the Sick* speak of a reality that every believer encounters in his or her life. The "General Introduction" goes on to say that "Christians feel and experience pain as do all other people; yet their faith helps them to grasp more deeply the mystery of suffering and to bear their pain with greater courage."[137] But the experience of suffering and illness can challenge faith and make hope elusive. It is only human to ask such questions as: "Why me?" "Where is God?" "How will I deal with this?" "What has this to do with Christ's suffering?" Answers to these questions may not come easily or in the early stages of illness. As the believer wrestles with his or her human situation they will move to another level of meaning that is rooted in the realization that their suffering and illness is imbued with the redemptive suffering of Christ himself. This is a moment of transformation. It transforms the human sense of meaninglessness to the meaningfulness that Jesus bestowed on all human conditions, especially the brokenness of life, by his cross and Resurrection.

---

135. See Walter Kasper, *Mercy: The Essence of the Gospel and the Key to Christian Life* (Mahwah, NJ: Paulist Press, 2013), 163.

136. PCS, 1.

137. PCS, 1.

The experience of suffering and illness can challenge our faith and make hope elusive.

His invitation to take up our cross was not an invitation to be burdened by pain or suffering; but a promise that we would move beyond the human condition to the joy, peace and serenity of being one with him in all things. "In the cross of Christ not only is the redemption accomplished through suffering, but also human suffering itself has been redeemed."[138] There is nothing that is not redeemable through the Paschal Mystery of Jesus Christ; the believer is called to surrender to that truth, to trust what is professed by faith. As Pope John Paul II said, "one can say that with the passion of Christ all human suffering has found itself in a new situation."[139]

Crosses abound in our lives, and suffering is not optional.[140] Jesus lived through his own suffering, and we can be assured that he knows our suffering and speaks with compassion, "Come to me, all you that are weary and are carrying heavy burdens, and I will give you rest. Take my yoke upon you and learn from me; for I am gentle and humble in heart, and you will find rest for your souls."[141] As Paul reflects on his sufferings in the name of Jesus Christ he can say, "Now I rejoice in my sufferings for your sake."[142]

138. *Salvifici doloris*, 19.
139. *Salvifici doloris*, 19.
140. Kenny, 165.
141. Matthew 11:28–29.
142. Colossians 1:24.

Not only does the individual struggle to integrate human suffering with Christian hope, so too the whole Church is called upon to take a stand on suffering in a world that often attempts to mask the reality of suffering and to eliminate the inevitability of pain. The Church proclaims that suffering and death itself do not have the last word for the believer. In her pastoral care of the sick the Church articulates the reality of and the experience of suffering and declares that suffering has meaning that is profoundly rooted in the suffering of Christ and in the relationship between his suffering and that of individuals. In her ministerial witness to the compassion of Christ, the Church, through her rituals, signs, and gestures lifts up the human condition to the level of grace and meaning. "Pain demands a response, while suffering demands an interpretation."[143]

The challenge for individuals who suffer, and for the Church that takes care of all her members, especially those who are sick and dying, is at the heart of the rites as they mediate the healing mercy of God. The Church's rites state that the sick and the dying possess an "inestimable value before God and people"[144] and they are counted among the beloved of the Father.

> Yet as we lean on God's mighty arm, we know that God can make a way out of no way, can comfort the sister bent double with the pain of cancer, not by chemotherapy but by the tender touch of the Holy Spirit. We know that God can strengthen the brother shaking scared of open heart surgery scheduled the next day, by the story of Jesus' passion told softy in the hospital room. We know that God can heal the hollow-faced, fever-racked son or daughter who is fighting HIV at every gasping breath, by a balm from Gilead. And we Roman Catholics, deeply sacramental people, know that this healing touch of God, this Spirit of comfort and this story of Christ's passion, are part of the mystery of salvation that is celebrated in the sacrament of the anointing of the sick.[145]

---

143. Joseph A. Selling, *Moral Questioning and Human Suffering: In Search of a Credible Response to the Meaning of Suffering* (Leuven, Belgium: Peeters, 1989).

144. Morrill, 140.

145. Richard McCarron, "Anointing the Sick," *Plenty Good Room* 5, no. 5 (January/February 1998): 3.

Frequently Asked Questions

1.   In what ways can the parish community be more involved with the rites of the sick?

First, it is helpful to remember that when a person is sick they may not be interested in a great number of visitors, whether they are at home or in a health care institution. The pastoral care team of the parish is really the representative outreach of the parish to the sick. The parish is vicariously connected to the sick through those who take up this ministry on behalf of the whole faith community.

A second issue concerns privacy. Some sick persons prefer to keep their health condition private, and pastoral ministers and others who may know of the person's illness need to respect this request. If the person agrees to let their name be mentioned in the Universal Prayer at Sunday and weekday Masses then that should be done without divulging their specific illness. Some parishes provide a list of those to be prayed for in the weekly bulletin; this allows everyone to include the sick in their daily prayer.

Parishioners can be invited to sign "get well" or "we're thinking of you" cards that can be taken to the sick person(s) by the pastoral care visitors. Such hand-written notes can be a cheerful gift for the sick. Many parishes have a "Prayer Shawl" ministry.[1] This involves a number of parishioners who meet on a regular basis and knit shawls that are given to the sick as a reminder that they are embraced in the prayer of the community during their time of illness. Usually a prayer card is attached to the shawl when it is delivered. Those who make these shawls also spend time in prayer when they get together. Like all ministries it is a way for people to nourish their own spiritual well-being and to connect their ministry through prayer to the Lord's ministry of compassion.

If the rites of the sick, especially the rite of anointing, are celebrated for the residents of a health care institution as a communal celebration, it may be possible for the time and place to be published in the parish bulletin. In this way members of the parish could set aside a moment of prayer at that

---

1.   Instructions for prayer shawls are found here: www.shawlministry.com/instructions.html.

Pastoral ministers may bring companion animals to visit those who are sick and homebound.

time for those persons; or, if possible join them for the liturgy in the chapel or prayer room of the institution. From time to time the parish may schedule a healing service during which there would be special prayers for all the sick in the parish, whether they would be present or not. The parish could also designate one weekday Mass a month, for example the first Saturday of every month, with the intention of praying for all who are sick. If a group in the parish comes together to pray the Rosary they might consider doing so on those days that acknowledge the sick.[2]

Some parishes are involving parishioners and their pets. Science now points to the calming effects that animals have upon people in reducing stress and anxiety as well as providing comfort.[3] Pet guardians whose animals pass the necessary certification may bring these animals to hospice care, hospitals, nursing homes, and so on, for scheduled visits. This is becoming very common in health care institutions and could easily be implemented in the parish setting.[4]

2. Refer to those days listed in question 12.
3. Refer to the Center for Disease Control and Prevention: www.cdc.gov/healthypets /health-benefits/index.html.
4. Visit the website of Pax Christi parish for more information: www.paxchristi.com /contentpages/43707/e7b2386e-c0ee-4c1b-b9fa-c39d5ba0b5ea/PaxPets-PetVisitMinistry.aspx.

2. How does HIPAA affect the rites of the sick and praying for the sick?

HIPAA, the Health Insurance Portability and Accountability Act, is a federal law passed by the United States Congress in 1996. HIPAA instituted national standards for the protection of consumers and client information. It applies particularly to health care providers—hospitals, public health departments, medical professionals, insurance companies, labs, home care companies, and surgery centers. In 2013, HIPAA was amended to cover concerns around Protected Health Information (PHI) and to provide further privacy and security reg-

HIPPA also protects the privacy of including the names of those who are sick in the Universal Prayers. Always seek permission.

ulations over the personal health information of patients. The law regulates what information on a patient's health situation can be shared, including past and current information, how it can be shared, and to whom it can be shared.

Although HIPAA is designed primarily to apply to employees of health care institutions, the regulations affect the role of pastoral care ministers and visitors to the sick when the sick person is being cared for in any health care institution. The fundamental premise of HIPAA is that a sick person has the right to share or withhold information on their illness. However, there are exceptions allowed for the health care provider.[5]

Since the regulations are designed to protect the privacy of the patient, it is the prerogative of the patient to share any information with others, outside the health care provider. This includes the sharing of information about diagnosis, treatment, and related information with pastoral care ministers or visitors. This means those who are from outside the health care

---

5. Under the Consent Rule of HIPAA the provider can use the health information for the purpose of Treatment, Payment, and Operations (TPO). For all other uses the provider must have the consent of the patient. For additional information, refer to this website: https://www.hhs.gov /hipaa/index.html.

institution, such as pastoral staff or volunteers from a parish. Those who are employed as members of the pastoral care team of the institution are bound by HIPAA and cannot share patient information with outside pastoral care visitors without the patient's consent. Obviously, the patient has more freedom to divulge information to others than do members of the staff. If the pastoral visitor is a volunteer acting under the auspices of the health care institution, in conjunction with the institution's chaplaincy pastoral care team, or volunteer office, then they are bound by HIPAA.

Another issue is obtaining permission from the patient to share their information with non–health care providers, for example family members and friends. As a result of HIPAA, many institutions have a consent form that the patient signs as part of the in-take process. This form, known by different names, includes communication choices, namely the names and contact information for those individuals authorized by the patient to receive information about their health situation. These contacts may include the patient's pastor or other pastoral care individual. Even in that situation the patient has the right to withhold some aspects of their health situation. Then the institution's staff, whether chaplain or medical personnel, should have the verbal permission from the sick person to reach out to their home parish or congregation.

Health care institutions no longer provide open access to patient information, for example in a file at the information desk. In the past, these files often provided information on the person's age, gender, background, and current diagnosis. In some ways, this was helpful information before the pastoral visitor walked into the sick person's room. However, this is precisely the type of information that is now considered protected and thus unavailable without patient consent. Although this might cause some initial frustration for the pastoral care visitor, the spirit of HIPAA is safeguarded, namely the rights of the patient and subsequent restricted access to their health information to a need-to-know basis. Some hospitals do provide for approved clergy (that is, those whom the patient has requested) to have access to the names of patients from specific parishes or religious traditions in the spiritual care office. It is always advisable to check with the hospital regarding the policy in this regard.

Pastoral care visitors, including clergy, should always be mindful of the importance and constraints of confidentially whenever they are dealing with members of their respective congregations, thereby respecting the dignity and wishes of the sick person. Pastoral visitors who visit residents in assisted living and long term settings should also be aware of any policies that relate to the matter of confidentiality. The simplest approach is to ask the sick person one or more key questions about sharing information. Examples of such questions would be:

- Do you want your name included in prayers for the sick at public liturgies?
- Do you wish to receive other visitors from your parish or congregation?
- Do you wish to receive the Sacraments of Reconciliation or Anointing of the Sick while you are in this institution?

The Rite of Anointing does not require detailed information about the sick person's condition; in most cases, the fact that they have been placed in an institution for a period of time because of illness would be a sufficient sign that they are eligible for anointing.

If a parish has a group of pastoral visitors who regularly visit members in health care institutions, then they should arrange for an orientation session with the pastoral care team of the institution so that they understand the policies and practices that apply under HIPAA.[6]

3. In what ways can more private celebrations of the rite (that is, those in which there is a very small number of people) be more communal?

Unless there is an urgent need to celebrate rites for the sick at short notice, the pastoral minister should make an effort to schedule the celebration when other persons can be present. Of course, the number of people will depend on the actual location of the sick person. A private home will usually have more available space than a hospital, unless the person can be moved to a hospital chapel or prayer room. Family members, nursing staff, and close friends can be invited, always being attentive to the wishes and the condition of the sick. The sick person as well as those who are present may be invited to participate in the rite by reading the Scripture passage and the intercessions. The pastoral minister should also invite all present to respond to the prayers, as well as to the Litany of Saints when it is part of the rite. In addition to the sick person, others may receive Holy Communion. If the pastoral minister is

---

6. Refer to these resources from the National Association of Catholic Chaplains regarding pastoral care and HIPAA: https://www.nacc.org/resources/chaplaincy-care-resources /pastoral-care-and-hipaa/.

able to chant a psalm, those present can participate in the refrain. The rubrics suggest that those who are present extend their hands in blessing; they may also be invited to make the Sign of the Cross on the sick person.

4. Are there rites for the sick that are not found in *Pastoral Care of the Sick* and what are they used for?

The *Order of Christian Funerals*

The *Order of Christian Funerals* includes the various rites that accompany the burial of a loved one. The presumption of the funeral rites is that a person has died and the family is now concerned with the preparation for and the celebration of the funeral liturgy. Prior to the funeral liturgy there may be an opportunity for mourners to gather for a time of prayer. The funeral rites provide the "Related Rites and Prayers,"[7] "Prayers after Death,"[8] and "Gathering in the Presence of the Body."[9] The pastoral notes of the rite assume that the family has already moved from the actual moment of death and is now dealing with the necessary preparations for a funeral liturgy. Prayers after Death provide "a model of prayer that may be used when the minister meets with the family following death."[10] Ordinarily, this pastoral visit happens sometime after the time of death, and may take place in the hospital or institution, in a parish office, in the home of a family member, or at the funeral home. The prayers that are provided could certainly be used by the pastoral minister who might have been present at the time of death, although it is unlikely that they would bring the *Order of Christian Funerals* when visiting a sick person, even if the person is dying. Prayers for the Dead in *Pastoral Care of the Sick*[11] are similar and as appropriate as those in *Order of Christian Funerals*. Gathering in the Presence of the Body is intended for use after the body has been prepared for the funeral and when the family members gather. Usually this gathering takes place in a funeral home or in a suitable place within the church where the funeral liturgy is to be celebrated. This rite is different from the Vigil for the Deceased and is intended for the prayerful support of the immediate family. In this situation the pastoral minister

---

7. See OCF, 98–100.
8. See OCF, 101–108.
9. See OCF, 109–118.
10. OCF, 101.
11. See PCS, 223–231.

needs to be attentive to the grief of the mourners and may make adaptations to the rite depending on cultural attitudes and practices.[12] As with the rites in the *Pastoral Care of the Sick*, the purpose of this rite is to offer consolation to the mourners and to call to mind the saving mercy of God for those who have been called into eternal life.

The *Rite of Christian Initiation of Adults*

The *Rite of Christian Initiation Adults* provides a Rite for the Christian Initiation of a Person in Danger of Death.[13] The pastoral notes indicate that this short rite can be used for persons, whether catechumens or not, who are in danger of death but are not at the point of death and so are able to hear and answer the questions involved.[14] The full rite is not exactly "short" as it includes the Sacrament of Baptism, Confirmation, and Viaticum. In this way it is similar to the Rite for Christian Initiation for the Dying in *Pastoral Care of the Sick*.[15] If the Sacrament of Confirmation is to be celebrated, only a priest is allowed to do so. A deacon or lay person may baptize and give Holy Communion. If, however, death is imminent, the pastoral minister, whether a priest, deacon, or lay person, may use the shorter rite which includes only the pouring of water with the baptismal formula. If the person who is dying is a child then the Rite of Baptism is celebrated in the usual way. If the child's death is imminent then the minister uses the short form that includes only the pouring of the water and the words of the baptismal formula.

Holy Communion and Worship of the Eucharist outside Mass

Holy Communion and Worship of the Eucharist outside Mass provides commentary and explanations of various rites, rubrics, and practices associated with the worship of Eucharist apart from the Mass. It provides the Rite of Distributing Holy Communion outside Mass (a longer[16] and shorter version[17]) and the Administration of Communion and Viaticum to the Sick by an

---

12. See OCF, 109.
13. See RCIA, 370–399.
14. See RCIA, 370.
15. See PCS, 275-296.
16. See Holy Communion and Worship of the Eucharist outside Mass (HCWEOM), 26–41.
17. See HCWEOM, 42–53.

Extraordinary Minister (a longer[18] and shorter version[19]).

The instructions in *Holy Communion and Worship of the Eucharist outside Mass* generally reiterate those found in other documents, for example, *The Roman Missal* and the *Universal Norms on the Liturgical Year and the Calendar*. Although the general norm is that Holy Communion may be given outside Mass on any day and at any hour[20] there are particular references for those who are sick that do not apply to others. On Holy

Communion may be given outside Mass in the home of the sick person.

Thursday, Communion may be given only during Mass, unless it is taken to a sick person. On Good Friday, Communion may be given only during the celebration of the Passion of the Lord, except for one who is sick. And on Holy Saturday, Communion may be given to the sick only as Viaticum.[21]

Although the place for giving Communion outside of Mass is ordinarily in a church or oratory where the Eucharist is regularly celebrated or reserved, Communion may also be given in other places, including the home of the sick person[22] or in a health care institution. The sick person may receive under both kinds, if they are able, and the transport of the Blessed Sacrament, whether as consecrated bread or wine, must be done reverently and securely. The elderly, and those suffering from any kind of infirmity, as well as those who take care of such persons are not obligated to observe a time of fast before receiving Communion.[23]

The celebration of Viaticum follows the norms found in the *Pastoral Care of the Sick*, chapter 5.[24]

---

18. See HCWEOM, 54–63.
19. See HCWEOM, 64–67. The distribution of Viaticum is found at HCWEOM, 68–78.
20. See HCWEOM, 16.
21. See HCWEOM, 16.
22. See HCWEOM, 18.
23. See HCWEOM, 24.
24. See PCS, 197–211. *The Book of Blessings* also includes rites for the sick.

5. What type of training should parishes provide ministers of care or extraordinary ministers of Holy Communion for the sick and homebound?

The training of pastoral care ministers and for those who bring Communion to the sick should cover two principal areas: practical issues for the exercise of the ministry and a formative segment on sacramental theology.

The first segment should include familiarity with the order of the rites for visiting the sick and for Communion to the sick as outlined in the *Pastoral Care of the Sick*. The pastoral minister should be familiar enough with these rites to be able to prepare the rite, being aware of whatever adaptations might be made, and choosing the prayers and readings when options are offered in the rite. The practical part of pastoral training should also include formation on presiding at a liturgical celebration. The pastoral minister should also be familiar with the additional rites that, although less likely to occur, are nonetheless part of pastoral care. These rites are included in chapter 8 of *Pastoral Care of the Sick*, Rites for Exceptional Circumstances. One of the rites is for baptizing in case of an emergency.

In addition to the practical aspects of this ministry, pastoral ministers should receive an introduction to the theology of the Sacraments of Eucharist and Anointing of the Sick. Although the lay pastoral minister cannot anoint, he or she should be familiar with the theology that informs the Church's tradition and practice of anointing the sick. The more the pastoral minister understands about the sacraments of Eucharist, including Viaticum, and the Anointing of the Sick, the better they are equipped to assist the sick and the dying.

Some diocesan liturgy offices require that ministers of care participate in training sessions and be commissioned before they are permitted to take up this ministry and give Communion to the sick. The parish coordinator of pastoral care should consult with the diocesan office to inquire what diocesan norms are in place for this ministry. Also, health care institutions may require parishes to provide an approved list of those who visit residents on behalf of the parish. This latter precaution may be part of the regulations associated with HIPAA.

6. What rites of the sick can be celebrated at Mass?

The Rite of Anointing and the Rite of Viaticum can be celebrated within Mass. *The Roman Missal* provides two ritual Masses in the section "For Various Needs and Occasions: For Anointing and for the Dying." Both Masses include prayers that are proper for the respective occasion. These ritual Masses are a different celebration than a Eucharistic liturgy that is celebrated as a Sunday or weekday liturgy during which either of these rites might be inserted. A ritual Mass is one in which the readings, prayers, intercessions, and music are focused on the particular pastoral situation. In other words, it is celebrated for the sick and with the sick present; or for the dying and with the dying present. Some parishes include the Anointing of the Sick during a Sunday or weekday Mass. In those instances, the short form for anointing is used and the prayers and readings proper to the day are used. On a weekday in Ordinary Time, the ritual Mass may be used.

The celebration of ritual Masses is not permitted during the Sacred Paschal Triduum; on the solemnities of Christmas, Epiphany, Ascension, Pentecost, Corpus Christi; or on a solemnity that is a Holyday of Obligation. The ritual Mass for Viaticum or the ritual Mass of the Holy Eucharist are also excluded on the Sundays of Advent, Lent, and Easter Time, on solemnities, Ash Wednesday, and the weekdays of Holy Week.[25]

7. In what ways can the Sunday liturgy and parish life be connected to those rites celebrated with the homebound or those in institutions?

The primary minister of the pastoral care of the sick is, of course, the Church, especially the local community of the faithful. When the Eucharistic community gathers to celebrate on Sunday she is always conscious of those members who are not able to be present. In a broad sense, the words of dismissal "Go and announce the Gospel of the Lord" is a commissioning of all to extend the ministry of the Lord to everyone. Other ways that the Sunday assembly can connect with those who are absent could include the following:

- Dismiss the pastoral care ministers prior to the final dismissal.
  This action points out to the assembly that those who are absent are vicariously present in the thoughts and prayers of their brothers and sisters, and are connected through the ministry of the pastoral visitors. The consecrated hosts are taken from those that are presented and consecrated during the Liturgy of Eucharist, thus underlining the fact that both those present and those who are not share in the spiritual bond of the Eucharist.

---

25. See PCS, 184.

- The sick should also be included in the intercessions of the Universal Prayer. If the sick are mentioned by name then the pastoral minister should be sure that the sick person(s) has agreed to have their name publicized in this way. Some parishes also place the names of the sick in the Sunday bulletin. Again, this needs the prior approval of the individual(s).

- Perhaps once or twice a year a member of the pastoral care team could offer a reflection at the Sunday liturgy, explaining the ministry and describing how it nourishes both those who are visited and those who go to visit the sick of the parish. This is also a good time to invite others to join this ministry. The reflection should take place following the Prayer after Communion.[26]

> The entire Church is made present in the community . . . assembled to pray for those to be anointed.
>
> —*Pastoral Care of the Sick,* 105

Those who are homebound or in health care institutions can keep in touch with the life of the parish through the Sunday bulletin and other printed material that describes programs and events in the parish. Pastoral care visitors should make a point of taking this material with them.

Some parishes have live-streaming broadcasts and/or podcasts of the Sunday liturgy. For those who are tech savvy these connections can be very rewarding.

8. How serious must the situation be in order for a person to be anointed?

Through the celebration of the sacrament the Church supports the sick in their struggle against illness and continues Christ's messianic work of healing.[27] The pastoral notes of *Pastoral Care of the Sick* offer the following in determining who should be anointed:[28]

- Those of the faithful whose health is seriously impaired by sickness or old age. An anointing can take place at the beginning of an illness that appears to be serious. There is no stipulation that anointing should wait

---

26. See RS, 74.
27. See PCS, 98.
28. See PCS, 8–12.

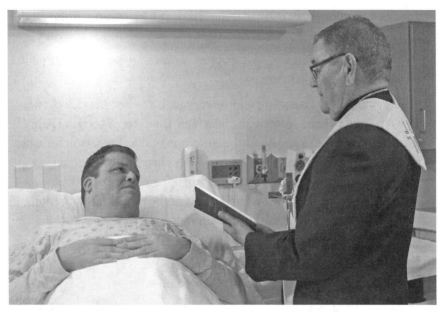
A person may be anointed before surgery; the reading of Scripture is an important part of the ritual.

until the illness has significantly progressed. However, the Sacrament of Anointing is not intended for a minor illness, such as a seasonal cold.[29]

- Those who recover from illness but who subsequently fall ill, or if during an illness their condition deteriorates after a previous anointing.

- A sick person may be anointed before surgery whenever a serious illness is the reason for the surgery.

- Elderly people may be anointed if they have become notably weakened even though no serious illness is present. It should be noted that old age is not so much a sickness, but rather a condition in which deteriorating health through length of years can constitute an intrinsic threat to life.[30]

- Children may be anointed if they have sufficient use of reason to be strengthened by the sacrament. Here the phrase "use of reason" is not based on chronological age but on the child's awareness that something

---

29.   At the same time it can be said that the seriousness of an illness can vary with different people, depending on other health issues one may have. What might be a minor sickness for one could be a serious condition for another. Pastoral judgement may be needed, and if necessary a consultation with the primary care physician.

30.   See comment on this point in the United States Bishops' Committee on the Liturgy, Newsletter XV, March/April 1979

good is taking place, namely that the "healing Christ is reaching out to touch the child."[31]

- If a person has been anointed during an illness and death is imminent, they are to receive Viaticum.

- "The sacrament of anointing may be repeated: a. when the sick person recovers after being anointed and, at a later time, becomes sick again; b. when during the same illness the condition of the sick person becomes more serious. In the case of a person who is chronically ill, or elderly and in a weakened condition, the sacrament of anointing may be repeated when, in the pastoral judgement of the priest, the condition of the sick person warrants the repetition of the sacrament."[32]

- Since "some types of mental illness are now classified as serious . . . those who are judged to have a serious mental illness and who would be strengthened by the sacrament may be anointed."[33]

- Those who have lost the use of reason, or have lapsed into unconsciousness may be anointed if, as Christian believers they would have requested it were they in control of their faculties.[34]

- Those in danger from some external cause, such as war, natural disaster, sentence of execution, or surgery unrelated to a dangerous illness should not be anointed.

- Those who have died should not be anointed; instead prayers for the deceased and for the mourners are appropriate.

The pastoral notes from the *Pastoral Care of the Sick* also make reference to who should not be anointed, apart from the note above stating that one who has died should not be anointed. It has become a common practice for pastoral ministers to invite all who wish to be anointed to come forward during those ritual Masses of anointing or during those communal liturgies, such as a weekday or Sunday Mass, where anointing is inserted into the liturgy of the day. The pastoral notes of the rite refer to this "practice of indiscriminately anointing numbers of people"[35] and state that such a practice is to be avoided.

---

31. Gusmer, 84.
32. PCS, 102.
33. PCS, 53.
34. See Gusmer, 84.
35. PCS, 108.

9. In what ways can we provide a more prayerful environment in hospitals and institutions in which there might be difficulty accessing the patient?

The pastoral notes from *Pastoral Care of the Sick* frequently refer to the condition of the sick person as a determining factor in the celebration of the pertinent rites and a reason for any adaptations that need to be made. It seems logical to include in that "condition" not only the person's medical status but also the physical setting or environment. First, the pastoral minister needs to use common sense in adapting to the given environment and adjusting the manner in which a rite is done. Monitors, intravenous tubes, life support systems, and so on, are

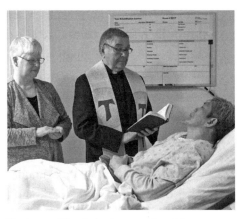

The focus of the rite is always on the sick person.

not incidental; they are there for a reason. They cannot be removed or switched off. The focus of the Church's rites is always on the person, whatever their condition and wherever they might be. The first concern is how to extend to the sick person a measure of comfort and assurance, in other words, to bring a ray of spiritual goodness into their life.

The pastoral minister should inform the professional staff what he or she needs to do, being respectful of the medical issues and the good will of the attending staff. Unusual circumstances call for special accommodations. The prayer of the Church will find its way and achieve its purpose in any human situation.

10. How do we minister to those who have highly contagious diseases?

Over the past several years, there have been remarkable advances in many areas of health care, including prevention, methods for alleviating illness, and in understanding the complex issues associated with illness. The subject of contagious diseases is among those that have benefited from such developments. Perhaps the first task of the pastoral minister is to be informed about some of the basic issues surrounding these illnesses, their characteristics, and their effect on the sick. This should be a topic of training sessions that are offered and possibly required by parishes.

Because of the issue of confidentiality, the health care staff may not be able to inform the pastoral care visitor of a person's specific illness.[36] If they require visitors to put on a breathing mask, hospital gown, and/or hygienic gloves, then the pastoral care person needs to do that as well. Also, ask the nursing staff what to do or what to avoid during the visit. For example, can the person swallow? Is it safe to touch the person? Should anything that the sick person touches be discarded? If the person suffers from a contagious disease then the health care staff, who are attending the person on a regular basis, will know the best way for the visitor to be helpful for the sick, and safe for themselves and for the sick person.

If a sick person has a contagious illness this information will be posted either on the door to their room or inside the room. The term used for this is Contact Restrictions (CR) and the sign may include both words and a symbol. The pastoral care visitor should first discuss the situation with nursing staff to discover what restrictions are in place and what policies apply to outside visitors. The other source of information is the institution's chaplain. The pastoral care visitors, including clergy, should not assume that they can bypass hospital policies in this situation.

11. When preparing healing Masses, what prayer texts and readings are used?

Pastoral Care of the Sick provides many options for the prayer texts and readings for healing Masses. In addition to those that are included in the outline of the respective rites, there is a range of options in part three of the ritual text: "Readings, Responses, and Verses from Sacred Scripture." Other Scripture readings may be selected from the *Lectionary for Mass*, "For the Pastoral Care of the Sick and Dying"[37] and "For Viaticum."[38] The parish liturgy team should consider the pastoral circumstances for the healing Mass, such as, the liturgical season, the focus that the homilist wishes to address, the condition of those who will be anointed, and any language or cultural aspects that will be included in the celebration. Since music is also a liturgical text, the music minister(s) will make selections based on similar considerations.

---

36. Refer to question 2 concerning HIPAA.
37. See *Lectionary for Mass*, 790–795.
38. See *Lectionary for Mass*, 796–800.

12. Are particular days to be avoided when scheduling healing Masses?

The pastoral notes in *Pastoral Care of the Sick* provide the norms that govern the times for the celebration of healing Masses. The ritual Mass for Anointing of the Sick is not permitted during Holy Week; on the solemnities of Christmas, Epiphany, Ascension, Pentecost, Corpus Christi; or on any solemnity that is a Holyday of Obligation. The ritual Mass is also excluded on the Sundays of Advent, Ash Wednesday, the Sundays of Lent, and the Sundays of Easter Time.[39]

13. In what ways can we encourage parish participation at healing Masses?

If a parish enjoys a strong bond of community and has a vital sense of herself as Church, then parish members will participate with energy and devotedness in the liturgies of anointing. It is important to provide information about the healing Mass well ahead of time so the necessary arrangements can be made for those to be anointed, such as transportation, the presence of care givers, and family members. The parish liturgy team will want to provide for the usual liturgical ministries, possibly scheduling additional ministers of hospitality.

Prior to the Mass of healing, parishioners can be reminded of how they share in the ministry of Jesus Christ by caring for and praying for the sick among them. This is the ministry of the Church, and as members of the local Church they are called to accompany the sick by their presence, in their love, and in their prayers. This encouragement for participation applies both to Sunday and weekday celebrations of healing Masses. A special invitation should be extended to all those who work in the field of health care, even if they are not directly involved with any of those being anointed. Young people in the parish, perhaps those preparing for Confirmation, may be invited to act as greeters for the celebration. The parish youth group may be asked to arrange for some hospitality after

> It is . . . fitting that all baptized Christians share in this ministry of mutual charity within the Body of Christ by doing all that they can to help the sick.
>
> —*Pastoral Care of the Sick*, 33

---

39. See PCS, 134.

the liturgy. Students in the parish school or in faith formation classes may prepare greeting cards or colorful posters that can be given to the sick as a memento of the celebration. The names of the sick may be included in the intercessions of the Universal Prayer; for the sake of privacy, only first names should be used. Once the liturgy team unlocks its imagination there may be other ways to encourage liturgical participation.

14. How does the anointing itself take place during Mass?

The two most common options for the Rite of Anointing is to have those being anointed come forward in a manner similar to the Communion procession. The assigned ministers of hospitality should assist with this if caregivers or family members are not present. A second option is for the minister

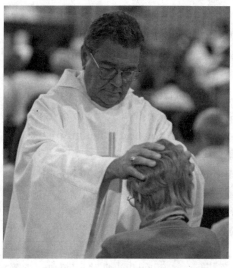

Seating arrangements should allow for the sick to find a place in the midst of the assembly.

to go to the place where the sick are seated. This can work well when an empty row is available in front of those to be anointed to accommodate the passage of the minister. Or, those to be anointed may be seated on the end of each pew. In this case, the ministers can walk down the aisle and anoint those seated at the end of the pews. In most cases, a combination of these options may work best. Seating arrangements should allow for the sick to find a place in the midst of the assembly, thus avoiding the rather inhospitable designation of a section "for the sick."

15. Are there other healing liturgies that do not involve anointing?

The compassionate care of the Church for all her members extends to every human experience of physical and mental illness, times of distress, spiritual anxiety, all those moments in life that create a sense of "dis-ease." In those times the Universal Prayer, whether in the rites of the Church or in other forms of prayer can be very comforting and spiritually effective for those experiencing illness or feelings of anxiety in and about life itself. Apart from the sacramental rites of the Church there is no one collection of rituals for situations beyond anointing. The *Book of Blessings*, which is an official ritual text, offers numerous ritual blessings for a breadth of occasions, persons, objects, and organizations.[40]

Although the blessings of persons are not referred to as "healing rites," they can bring a certain healing of mind and spirit to persons.[41] Other rituals that might bring a measure of peace and healing to persons can be created by anyone. These rites can be led by anyone who is respected by those who participate and whose faith disposes them to act reverently and humbly in asking for the grace of the Lord upon the persons in need. These rites are rightly called sacramentals since they are done in the name of the Lord and invoke the Holy Spirit to bring divine grace to the human situation.

16. What limitations might present themselves for effective pastoral ministry of healing due to hospital rules and regulations?

It is helpful to remember that hospitals and other health care institutions are in the business of helping those who are sick to get better. Thus, the primary focus of the hospital staff is the comfort, care, and return to health of their patients. However, health care personnel are increasingly aware that a person's well-being is more than physical; it also includes emotional, spiritual, and mental issues. One general hospital uses the byline "we also treat the human spirit."

That being said, hospitals are very attentive to the spiritual needs of their patient residents. Most hospitals will have a pastoral care office and one or more chaplains and do their best to provide for the specific religious needs of their patients. Any regulations that are in place are intended to provide a safe and secure atmosphere for patients: for example, the hours for visitation, the number of visitors in a person's room at any one time, and the ability of the sick person to endure a lengthy ritual.

---

40. The *Book of Blessings* includes the Order for the Blessing of a Mother before Childbirth, Order for the Blessing of Parents after a Miscarriage, Orders for the Blessing of the Sick, Order for the Blessing of a Person Suffering from Addiction or from Substance Abuse, and Orders for the Blessing of a Victim of Crime or Oppression.

41. See those blessings related to health situations in the appendix of this book.

There are certain protocols that pastoral care visitors need to observe. These may appear to restrict the freedom of the pastoral minister to access parish members, but the positive purpose of the regulations outweigh the temporary inconvenience to the pastoral visitor. As pastoral ministers become accustomed to the policies and practices of the hospital these various regulations will not be limitations for pastoral care but rather helpful guidelines for their ministry.

17. Are there any issues with celebrating the sacramental rites or other prayers of healing with those who are not Catholic?

The issue of celebrating the sacraments with those who are not Catholic first must be understood within the Church's teaching on the sacraments. A sacrament is an act of Christ and of the Church through the Spirit. The celebration of a sacrament takes place in a particular community and is a sign of unity in faith, worship, and community. The sacraments are also a means for the building up of the spiritual life of the community of faith and are, especially the Eucharist, inseparably linked to the full ecclesial communion and its visible expression.

At the same time, the Catholic Church teaches that by Baptism members of other Churches and ecclesial communities are brought into a real, even if imperfect communion, with the Catholic Church. The sacramental bond of Baptism is a bond of unity that exists among all those who through it are reborn and it is directed toward acquiring the fullness of life in Christ.

In light of these two principles taken together the Catholic Church permits access to the Eucharist and to the Sacraments of Penance and the Anointing of the Sick for those who share its oneness in faith, worship, and ecclesial life. It also recognizes that in certain circumstances, by way of exception and under certain conditions, access to these sacraments may be permitted or even commended for Christians of other Churches and ecclesial communities.

The conditions under which a Catholic priest may administer the sacraments of Eucharist, Penance, and the Anointing of the Sick to a baptized person who is not Roman Catholic are the following:

- In danger of death, when the person is unable to have recourse for the sacrament desired to a minister of his or her own Church or ecclesial community.

- When they ask for the sacrament of their own accord.

- When they manifest Catholic faith in this sacrament and are properly disposed.[42]

In other cases, apart from danger of death, conferences of bishops may establish norms to cover situations of grave and pressing need that would take into consideration the previously mentioned conditions.[43] If a Catholic minister receives a request for one or more of the three sacraments noted, and there is no danger of death, then he should consult with the local bishop as to whether norms have been established permitting him to celebrate sacraments with a baptized person who is not a Roman Catholic.

It should be noted here that Catholic ministers may lawfully administer the Sacraments of Penance, Eucharist, and the Anointing of the Sick to members of the Eastern Churches who ask for these sacraments of their own free will and are properly disposed.[44]

18.   What considerations need to be made when anointing persons with disabilities?

The pastoral ministry of the Church is in imitation and continuation of the ministry of Jesus Christ. The compassion of Jesus and gestures of hospitality should shape the ministry of those in pastoral care. In recent years, pastoral leaders have become especially conscious of the rights of individuals with various abilities to have access to the liturgical life of the Church, by participating in ministries, having physical access to the church building, and being able to celebrate the

Pastoral staff should ensure that people with varying abilities have full access to the liturgical life of the church, including access to the church building.

---

42.   See the *Directory for the Application of Principles and Norms on Ecumenism* (DAP), 131; see also CCL, 844.4

43.   See DAP, 130.

44.   See DAP, 125.

sacraments. In the past several years, a number of civil and Church documents have addressed the issue of advocacy for persons with disabilities.[45]

The United States bishops' *Guidelines for the Celebration of the Sacraments with Persons with Disabilities* sets out the following norms:

- Since the Anointing of the Sick is properly celebrated only in the case of serious illness or in the case of debilitating old age, a disability in and of itself is never a reason to celebrate the sacrament.[46]

- Ordinarily the person to be anointed must have the "use of reason," but one may be anointed who, having lost the use of reason, would otherwise have asked to be anointed.[47]

- Because the sacrament is intended to strengthen and comfort the one who is anointed, cases of doubt are resolved in the favor of the person to be anointed.[48]

- Pastoral care ministers should be attentive to the person who is living with a particular ability, and not see them as "the disabled." Those who accompany a person with disabilities, whether a family member or care giver, should also be involved in the celebration of anointing. If the person is able to participate in the celebration in any way they should be encouraged to do so. If the parish schedules a communal celebration of the Anointing of the Sick, and if there are persons who require special accommodations such as accessibility to the church, then the liturgy team should see that such accommodations are provided.

19. How should one be anointed?

The rubrics for the Anointing of the Sick do not specify the manner of anointing. Nor do the rubrics state how the anointings are done in the Sacrament of Baptism. However, in the Sacrament of Confirmation the rubric notes that the bishop anoints the forehead of the one being confirmed with chrism in the form of a Cross. The gesture of anointing could be in the form of a cross or something like a smear or rubbing of the oil on the forehead and hands of the one being anointed. It was noted earlier that other parts of the body

---

45. See National Conference of Catholic Bishops, *Pastoral Statement on People with Disabilities* (1978); *Americans with Disabilities Act* [ADA] (1990); *Individuals with Disabilities Education Act* [IDEA] (1998); National Conference of Catholic Bishops, *Guidelines for the Celebration of the Sacraments with Persons with Disabilities* (1995).

46. See CCL, 1004.

47. See CCL, 1006.

48. See CCL, 1005.

may be anointed, for example the area of injury or pain. It can be assumed that the same gesture would be used in those situations. In the celebrations of the sacraments the Church makes use of various signs that can "express the sanctifying presence of God and man's gratitude toward his Creator."[49]

The use of oil in religious rituals carries a meaning from very ancient times of God's intervention in human affairs. From the anointing of kings and prophets, to the anointing of the sick in the early Church, to the anointings in Christian sacraments, the gesture of anointing is a holy thing. The amount of oil that is used can convey the generous compassion that God lavishes on those who are sick. The sense of touch can be very healing for a sick person and the gesture of anointing should be gentle, deliberate, and soothing. Although it may not be practical to use generous amounts of oil in every situation, the priest should avoid any semblance of efficiency or minimalism.

20. What are common abuses of the sacrament and how can these be avoided?

Perhaps the most common abuse of the Sacrament of Anointing is in the "practice of indiscriminately anointing numbers of people"[50] during communal celebrations. Perhaps the abuse is not so much in the actual anointing as in the open-ended invitation by a pastoral minister inviting "anyone who would like to be anointed to come forward." The Rite of Anointing is not a pious act similar to a communal celebration of the Rosary or the Stations of the Cross in which any devout person might participate. Just as the Sacrament of Reconciliation requires a confession of sin as the matter for the sacrament, so the Anointing of the Sick is for those who are seriously ill.[51] Another abuse is when a pastoral minister who is not ordained celebrates the Rite of Anointing or some form of an anointing rite without telling the person being anointed that it is not the sacrament. If the priest shortens the rite by omitting the Scripture reading and some or all the prayers for personal reasons, for example if he is in a hurry, this would constitute an abuse of the ritual act. If he says the formula for anointing and performs the double anointing, the sacrament would be valid; but the act of pastoral ministry would be inappropriate.

---

49. CCC, 1148.
50. PCS, 108.
51. Refer to question 8 for more information.

21. How can indiscriminate anointing be avoided in a communal setting?

The most obvious way to avoid the indiscriminate anointing of people when the anointing takes place in a communal setting, is for the pastoral minister, whether priest, deacon or other liturgical minister, to follow the pastoral notes when inviting people to come forward to be anointed.[52]

Although it may seem hospitable to invite "everyone" or "whoever wishes" to be anointed, such an invitation is not faithful to the pastoral intent or the liturgical theology of the sacrament. The pastoral minister could add further comment to assist people in discerning if their illness or situation is covered by the pastoral guidelines.

It will be helpful to publish these guidelines in the parish bulletin prior to the date of the celebration. Another way to offer catechesis on the sacrament is in the Sunday homily. There are several Sundays throughout the year when the Gospel relates one or more of the healing encounters in Jesus' ministry. Even if a communal anointing is not being scheduled for that Sunday, the homilist can offer liturgical catechesis on the Sacrament of Anointing of the Sick. In this way every member of the congregation is made aware of the theology and the pastoral norms of the sacrament. This information helps those who are sick, their family members, and care givers to make the appropriate decision in good faith about being anointed.

In the pastoral situation where an individual requests anointing, and if the priest is unsure of the need, then he can inquire about the person's illness. In this situation the pastoral notes are helpful: "A prudent or reasonably sure judgement, without scruple, is sufficient for deciding on the seriousness of an illness; if necessary, a doctor may be consulted."[53] In actual practice, most priests would trust that the person's request to be anointed is made in good faith and would anoint them.

In the matter of the actual celebration of the sacrament, the rubrics in the ritual text should be followed without omitting any of the elements of the respective rite. Since the pastoral notes allow for changes to the rite, for example omitting some prayers or using a shorter reading, based on particular circumstances, the priest should not, on his own, modify the rite without good reason.

---

52. See PCS, 9-13.
53. PCS, 8.

If it becomes known that a pastoral minister, who is not ordained, celebrates an anointing service (such as with charismatic groups), then he or she must inform the recipient that this was not the Sacrament of Anointing. The pastor or the pastoral care coordinator should caution, or even forbid this person from repeating such a ceremony. As part of the catechesis in a homily as noted above, it can be stated that the only minister of the Sacrament of Anointing is a priest or bishop.

Another form of catechesis is by making pamphlets available to any parishioner who is interested in this sacrament. A number of publishers provide such booklets at a minimum cost. The parish liturgy team could prepare a suitable handout or booklet that would include the pastoral notes from the ritual text, as well as pertinent information about the parish's pastoral care ministry. Pastoral care visitors could provide these to all those whom they visit and spend a few moments discussing the practice and the benefits of the sacrament with the sick person and others who are present with them.

22. How do we differentiate between sacramental anointing from charismatic healing groups who are using oil in "healing" prayer services?

The anointing rituals associated with "healing" services that are common with charismatic gatherings and sometimes are celebrated with retreat groups should not be confused with the Sacrament of the Anointing of the Sick. There are two characteristics that differentiate a healing service from the sacrament. First, the recipients are not gathered because they are sick but because they wish to pray together. Second, not everyone who performs the anointings is a priest or bishop. Although the healing service may appear similar to the sacramental Rite of Anointing, including prayers, readings, and the laying on of hands, the leaders of the gathering have an obligation to make it very clear that the healing ritual is not a celebration of the sacrament.

23. What should a minister do if a person who is not very ill wishes to be anointed?

When someone approaches a pastoral minister asking to be anointed, the minister should assume that the person does so in good faith. However, the Sacrament of Anointing is not a generic rite that can or should be applied to every human issue of anxiety or distress. The minister should spend a few

The Rite of Anointing should always bring the sick person comfort, peace, and strength.

moments in conversation with the person to determine what has initiated the request for anointing. It may be that a simple blessing is called for along with the assurance that the grace of the Lord is thus bestowed upon them to strengthen them and bring them peace of mind. It is also true that some illnesses can seem very serious for some persons but not considered as serious for others. People have different tolerance levels and different understandings of the seriousness of the illness. If the minister determines that the person's distress is serious and caused by illness, even if it might not normally be considered serious, then he may anoint. The intention of the sacrament is always to provide spiritual strength for the person and a sense of well-being in the Lord.

If a person comes forward at a healing Mass and the minister has some reservation as to whether they are seriously ill, he might engage the person in a brief conversation, if that seems appropriate in the circumstance. However, this is not the time for extended catechesis. In practice, the minister will assume that the person is ill and the symptoms are not so obvious. To avoid such a situation, the presider should always offer a brief explanation of the sacrament, including who should be anointed prior to the rite itself. The presider may invite those who will not be anointed to come forward and to indicate with some gesture that they wish to receive a blessing. Ordinarily, young children and infants should not be anointed in these situations.

24. The Rite of Exorcism is a service of healing. Who is it used for and when is it appropriate to use?

The Catholic Church authorizes the use of exorcism for those who are believed to be the victims of demonic possession. In the Rite of Exorcism the "Church asks publicly and authoritatively in the name of Jesus Christ that a person or object be protected against the power of the Evil One and withdrawn from his dominion."[54] Ordinarily an exorcism is performed as a remedial action

---

54.   CCC, 1673.

as compared to a preventive act and is "directed at the expulsion of demons or to the liberation from demonic possession through the spiritual authority which Jesus entrusted to his Church."[55]

The minister of the Rite of Exorcism is a priest who acts with the permission of the bishop.[56] The bishop may appoint a priest to perform exorcisms on a case-by-case basis; or he may establish an office of exorcist for the diocese. There must be moral certitude that an exorcism is warranted. This assessment will ordinarily involve a team of ministers with consultations from a medical doctor, a psychologist or a psychiatrist, a spiritual counsellor, and a priest. The reason for such a consultation is to distinguish between a psychological illness that requires a long-term intervention and an actual demonic possession.

The Rite of Exorcism is a rite of healing; it belongs in the realm of spiritual well-being and thus is addressed by the Church. The concern of medical science is with the mental and physical health of a person. There can be certain symptoms of illness similar to those of demonic possession, for example, severe distress, self-inflicted physical injury, lack of emotional control, and ravings of a religious nature, hence the necessity for a consultative conversation between professional care givers. In fact the guidelines that accompany the official rite state that a medical consultation must be done in order to rule out mental illness.

> The Church implores Christ the Lord and Savior and, relying on his strength, offers to the member of the faithful who is tormented or possessed a number of helps, so that he or she may be freed from torment or possession.
>
> —*Rite of Exorcism*, 105

The Latin text of the *Rite of Exorcism* was revised in 1999; the original rite dates from 1614. It is a sacramental of the Church, but is not a sacrament. Because of the infrequency of demonic possession in the western part of the Church, most parish priests do not have a copy of the *Rite of Exorcism*, and very few would have actually used the rite.[57] If a priest receives a request for an exorcism he should notify the appointed exorcist of his diocese or, if no one is in that office, he should contact the bishop directly.

---

55.   CCC, 1673; see also CCL, 1172.

56.   See CCL, 1172.

57.   The rite can be found online and anyone might then use the prayers of the rite. However, this can be a dangerous practice because of the impression it would give to others unfamiliar with the seriousness of the situation. Only a priest with the permission of his bishop can perform an exorcism.

Once the Rite of Exorcism has been performed and a positive situation results, the priest may suggest that the person celebrate the Sacrament of Reconciliation and/or the Anointing of the Sick.

25. How can parish catechesis differentiate between Last Rites and the possible need for the rites for the sick throughout the Christian life?

Although the revised Rite of the Anointing of the Sick has been part of the Church's liturgical practice since it was approved in 1972, there remains some popular understanding that the Last Rites, the name given to Extreme Unction, are associated with imminent death. The pastoral practice of the Church and the various efforts of catechesis have in fact changed this perception over time. However, continued catechesis is still needed. Homilies, bulletin announcements, and word-of-mouth information are helpful ways to inform people of the purpose of the Sacrament of Anointing of the Sick. Many parishes have a regular section in the bulletin that gives the basic information on the celebration of the sacraments, such as Baptisms, weddings, and the Anointing of the Sick. This is always helpful. When communal celebrations of healing Masses are scheduled, an extended announcement can be made on who can be anointed. The homilist can always speak about the benefits of the sacrament for those who, at different times during life, experience a serious illness. The proliferation of healing Masses in parishes has been its own form of catechesis as they remind people that anointing is not for those who are near death but for all those who struggle with sickness.

Sometimes it is helpful to briefly describe the history of the sacrament, indicating how the Church has always had a special concern for those who are sick and for the dying. And, as with the liturgical renewal in other areas of the Church, the pastoral care of the sick and the dying has also changed over the course of time. By emphasizing that the sacraments are for the living, the homilist can help people in their understanding of Viaticum as the sacrament that prepares the faithful for the final journey into eternal life. In fact, it is often a lack of understanding of Viaticum that is more prevalent. Any time there is a homily on the Eucharist, the homilist may reference the importance of Viaticum for those who are near death. The parish may prepare or purchase pamphlets on the Sacrament of the Anointing of the Sick and Viaticum and make these available for parishioners.

26. May Mass be celebrated with the sick and homebound in hospitals, institutions, homes, or other locations?

Pastoral Care of the Sick provides two rites in chapter 3 for Communion of the Sick. Both these rites are in the form of a Communion service, that is, a Liturgy of the Word with Communion. However, the pastoral notes do not explicitly forbid the celebration of Mass with the homebound, a seriously ill person in a nursing home or hospital, or one that is dying in their hospital room or home. The pastoral notes for the celebration of Viaticum, chapter 5, actually give preference for Viaticum to be celebrated within Mass,[58] and allow for the celebration of Mass with a dying person in their home or in an institution.[59]

However, because of limited arrangements in either location, and depending on the condition of the seriously ill or dying person, the Order of Mass may be simplified.[60] This might mean shortening the Scripture readings and the intercessions, omitting the Creed, using Eucharistic Prayer II, and omitting music. Whether Mass is celebrated in a home or an institution the site should be suitable for the celebration of Mass, with sufficient privacy for the persons involved, and making sure that the sick or dying person is able to participate, or at least be aware of what is taking place. When a priest is not available for the celebration of Mass, then a Communion service is always appropriate.

27. When worship teams gather throughout the year, how might they evaluate and discuss liturgies related to those who are ill?

The ministry of pastoral care is more than rubrics, presiding techniques, or schedules. Pastoral care is embedded in the stories that arise from the spiritual encounters that take place between those who minister and those to whom they minister. So often, those who are recipients of ministry are the ones who in turn minister to those who visit them. Keeping in mind the importance of confidentiality, pastoral ministers can learn a great deal about their ministry by sharing their experiences and insights with each other.

---

58. See PCS, 177.
59. See PCS, 178.
60. See PCS, 178.

At the same time it's always important to review and evaluate the work of ministry. It can be helpful by asking what worked well and what did not work. The answers can assist the pastoral ministers to make positive adjustments in the future.

Practical matters like scheduling, availability of the necessary information, and so on, should be reviewed on a regular basis. Other issues related to the actual celebrations include the following:

- Were the various liturgical ministries covered and were they done well at communal celebrations?
- Were there any issues with those who participated in the liturgy, such as accessibility needs, the availability of worship aids, and transportation needs?
- Was the liturgy too long considering the condition of the sick who were present?
- Was the selection of readings and music engaging and appropriate for participation by the whole assembly?

For those rites celebrated in homes or health care institutions other issues might be explored:

- Was any follow-up needed and how was that communicated to other ministers, for example, requests for the Sacrament of Penance or Anointing?
- Are participation booklets/worship aids/hymnals always available for the sick and for others who are present for the celebration?
- Are there issues related to hospital regulations and protocol? If so, who needs to assist with resolving those issues?

It's always a good idea to review the pastoral notes for the different rites to assess if the underlying spiritual and liturgical intent of the rites is unfolding in the actual celebrations. The many elements of *Pastoral Care of the Sick* offer a rich source for reflection as well as for the spiritual growth of the pastoral minister.

28. Can the Precious Blood be taken on a visit to a sick person?

The rite allows for the Precious Blood to be taken to the sick if they are unable to receive communion under the form of bread.[61] If the sick person is not present at the Eucharistic celebration then the Precious Blood is placed in the tabernacle until such time as the pastoral care visitor is ready to visit the sick person. Ordinarily this should not be an extended period of time as the consecrated wine will spoil. However, the *Norms for the Distribution and Reception of Holy Communion under Both Kinds in the Dioceses of the United States* do allow or the temporary reservation of the Precious Blood for the purposes of the sick. The document states the Precious Blood may never be reserved, "except for giving Communion to someone who is sick." When this is done "the Blood of the Lord is kept in a properly covered vessel and is placed in the tabernacle after Communion. . . . If some of the Precious Blood remains after the sick person has received Communion, it should be consumed by the minister, who should also see to it that the vessel is properly purified."[62] Once the pastoral care minister receives the consecrated bread or wine from the altar, or retrieves them from the tabernacle, they should go directly to the place of the sick person.

29. What is the proper way to transport the Blessed Sacrament?

Both the consecrated bread and the consecrated wine should be carried in a secure vessel. The container for consecrated bread is called a pyx. There isn't a readily available container for the Precious Blood and so the pastoral care minister will have to find one that is "closed in such a way as to eliminate all danger of spilling."[63] If some of the Precious Blood remains after the sick person receives Communion, then it should be consumed by the minister. The vessel is then purified in the same way as the Communion vessels used at Mass.

---

61. See PCS, 74.
62. *Norms for the Distribution and Reception of Holy Communion under Both Kinds in the Dioceses of the United States*, 54.
63. PCS, 74.

30. Must Holy Communion always be given when visiting the sick and homebound?

Pastoral Care of the Sick provides two rites for visits to the sick. Chapter 1 is a general rite and chapter 2 is for visits to a sick child. Neither of these rites includes Holy Communion. Chapter 3 provides the Rite for Communion to the Sick in Ordinary Circumstances and in a Hospital or Institution. The pastoral visitor should know ahead of time whether or not the sick person wishes to receive Communion since the pastoral visitor shouldn't carry the Blessed Sacrament on their person "just in case" the sick person or persons might want to receive Holy Communion. The visitor should also ask if there will be others present who will want to receive Holy Communion.

In addition to these rites, there isn't any reason why any member of the parish couldn't visit a sick person of the parish, provided the sick person is open to such a visit. This more informal visit is a good way for the parish to keep in touch with those who are sick and for the sick person to feel that they have not been forgotten.

31. Is Viaticum ever celebrated during Mass?

Pastoral Care of the Sick provides two rites for the celebration of Viaticum in chapter 5: within Mass and outside Mass. The Order of Mass is similar to any Eucharistic celebration and Viaticum is given during the Communion rite. The celebration may take place in the church or in any suitable place, such as a hospital chapel or the home of the sick person.

> The thing the Church needs most today is the ability to heal wounds and to warm the hearts of the faithful; it needs nearness, proximity. I see the Church as a field hospital after battle.
>
> —*Pope Francis*

32. Do the rites really need to be performed as prescribed?

The short answer is yes. The sacramental rites of the Church provide an order for the prayers, readings, and gestures of the rite and a certain rhythm that is suitable for most pastoral circumstances. The rite has both a theological integrity and a liturgical tradition that speak of the ecclesial nature of the liturgy. In other words, the rites are not personal or private acts; they belong to the whole Church and express the Church's embrace of her members through the respective sacramental rites. So, ordinarily, the rite should be celebrated as prescribed. However, the minister of the rite, whether ordained or lay, should be aware that the pastoral notes allow for adaptations based on the particular circumstances. These adaptations allow some flexibility and initiative on the part of the pastoral minister; however, adaptations should not be done in a way that allows a casual or personal disregard for the integrity of the rite in its given format.

33. What should be done with a host that someone spits out or is unable to swallow?

This situation can easily arise if the sick person has difficulty swallowing. The simple procedure is to place the host in a purificator (do not use a paper napkin) or in a small vessel of water. The pastoral minister should return the purificator or the vessel of water to the sacristy as soon as possible. The host from the purificator can be dissolved in water and the water poured into the sacrarium. Similarly, if the host has been placed in a vessel of water and has subsequently dissolved, then it should be poured into the sacrarium. Other suitable options include burning or burying the consecrated host. However, it is likely that the host will easily dissolve in water and using the sacrarium is the best option.

34. Can Holy Communion be administered through a feeding tube?

The issue of giving Communion through a feeding tube is first a medical concern before it is a liturgical concern. Ordinarily, there are two types of feeding tubes. One is inserted through a person's nose and is intended as a temporary measure. The other is inserted through a person's side and into the stomach; this is usually a more permanent arrangement.

Giving Communion with a consecrated host through a feeding tube is very risky and it is unlikely that a doctor would allow it simply because there is considerable risk of the host blocking the passage. A small portion of the host could be dissolved in water and then given through the feeding tube.

An alternative method is for a small portion of the host to be placed on the person's tongue where it will naturally dissolve and be swallowed by the sick person. In most cases when a person has a feeding tube they are still able to swallow a minimal amount of fluids, so a dissolved host will be allowed.

However, some sick persons have an NPO posted (*nil per os* or nothing by mouth). In that situation, they are not allowed to receive anything by mouth, including fluids. If however, the person is allowed to receive fluids by mouth then they may receive Holy Communion with the Precious Blood. In this case, a small amount can be given by mouth.[64] In every situation, the pastoral care minister should first check with the medical staff before using any option for Communion when there is a feeding tube present.

35. May anyone baptize in danger of death? If so, how is this done?

The ordinary ministers of Baptism are a bishop, priest, and deacon. In the case of necessity, anyone, even a nonbaptized person, with the required intention, can baptize.[65] The intention required is to will what the Church does when she baptizes,[66] namely, to impart the saving grace of God and to welcome the person into Christian faith. As noted in the commentary on the Rite for Christian Initiation for the Dying, the rite may be shortened depending on the condition of the dying person. The minimum required is the pouring of water accompanied by the Trinitarian formula, "**N.**, I baptize you in the name of the Father, and of the Son, and of the Holy Spirit."

If the dying person is a catechumen and it is known or can reasonably be assumed that they intended to be baptized, then Baptism can take place. If the dying person is a child and the parents or a family member are not present, and it is very likely that they would wish to have their child baptized, then Baptism can take place. If there is good reason to believe that the parents would not want their child to be baptized, for example because they are of a non-Christian faith tradition, then it would not be wise to baptize. Good intentions notwithstanding, it is not right to play God.

---

64. The precautions about bringing the Precious Blood to the sick person's home or hospital room as noted in question 29 should be followed.

65. See CCC, 1256, and CCL, 861.2.

66. See CCC, 1256 and CCL, 861.2.

Appendix: Preparing the Orders of Blessing

"The source from whom every good gift comes is God, who is above all, blessed for ever."

—*Book of Blessings*, 1

The celebration of blessings holds a privileged place among all the sacramentals of the Church for the pastoral benefit of the people of God. The invocation and conferral of blessings on persons and objects is part of the sanctifying ministry of the Church. Blessings call the faithful to praise God, encourage them to implore the protection of God, exhort them to seek the mercy of God by a holiness of life, and provide them with ways of praying that God will grant the favors that are asked for. Many blessings are directed to persons at various times and for various reasons during their life.

The practice of invoking God's blessing is a long standing tradition in the life of the Church. Blessings are praise of God for the many gifts of God's providence. At the same time they are an expression of faith on the part of those who seek God's blessing for their well-being and their spiritual

> The Church gives glory to God in all things and is particularly intent on showing forth his glory to those who have been or will be reborn through his grace.
>
> —*Book of Blessings*, 12

renewal. There are also blessings designed for the sanctification of places, times, and objects. These items can be seen as vehicles of the goodness in God's creation and signs for the faithful of the care that God has for all things.

The typical form of a blessing includes at least one reading from Scripture, a prayer of praise for the goodness of God, one or more petitions for God's assistance, and an opening and closing greeting and prayer that is proper to each blessing. The blessing may also include the sprinkling of holy water on the person, object, or place; the signing of the Cross on the person; the laying on of hands; and the use of incense. Since the blessing is in the form of an oration, the minister may extend his or her hands or clasp the hands of the person(s) being blessed, depending on the rubrics for the particular blessing.

The ministry of blessing belongs first to the bishop; one thinks of the blessing of the holy oils at the Mass of Chrism; then to a priest in the exercise of his ministerial service to the people of God. Some blessings may be given by a deacon, an instituted lector or acolyte, or a lay person, man or woman, depending on the rubric associated with the particular blessing.[67] Since blessings are part of the liturgy of the Church, the presence and participation of a community of faith is the preferred form of the celebration, and in some cases a communal celebration is obligatory.

Some blessings have a special relationship to the sacraments and may sometimes be joined with the celebration of Mass or to the celebration of the appropriate sacrament. Other liturgical celebrations, for example the Liturgy of the Hours, may be a suitable time for a blessing. Several blessings may be given in the same celebration and more than one person or object may be blessed in the same celebration.[68]

> The presence of the faithful is preferable, since what is done on behalf of any group within the community redounds in some way to the good of the entire community.
> —Book of Blessings, 16

Blessings that do not include the celebration of Mass or one of the sacraments may be celebrated in any appropriate place, for example a person's home, a hospital room, or the room of a health care residence. In each situation care should be taken that the liturgical nature of the blessing not be diminished, that proper devotion be maintained, and that the blessing not appear to be a casual exercise. The minister—if a bishop, priest, or deacon—may wear appropriate vesture, depending on the pastoral circumstance and the nature of the liturgy, such as an alb and stole.[69] A lay minister could wear an alb for a blessing.

In communal celebrations of blessings other ministers may participate. This includes ministers of hospitality to greet guests of the person(s) being blessed; for example, a wedding anniversary celebration or civic officials at the blessing of a site for a new church building. Readers can be scheduled for the Scripture proclamation and cantors, instrumentalists, and choir

---

67. See BB, 18.
68. See BB, 28–30.
69. See BB, 35–8.

members can lead the music. The parish liturgy team or liturgy coordinator will need to determine what preparations are needed such as providing worship aids, scheduling liturgical ministers, and if a social event will be part of the celebration (for this, the parish council should also be involved).

The following blessings might take place as part of the parish's ministry to the sick and other health care purposes and are found in the *Book of Blessings*:

- Orders for the Blessing of the Sick (chapter 2)
- Orders for the Blessing of a Person Suffering from Addiction or from Substance Abuse (chapter 2)
- Order for the Blessing of a Victim of Crime or Oppression (chapter 2)
- Order for the Blessing of Parents before Childbirth (chapter 1)
- Orders for the Blessing of a Mother before and after Childbirth (chapter 1)
- Orders for the Blessing of Parents after a Miscarriage (chapter 1)
- Distribution of Ashes to the Sick (chapter 52)

Orders for the Blessing of the Sick

The Orders for the Blessing of the Sick include three rites: one for the blessing of an adult and two for the blessing of a child (a long form and a short form). These blessings are related to the Rite for Visits to the Sick found in the *Pastoral Care of the Sick*. Both rites share the same intent: to express the compassionate care of the Church for those who are sick and to invoke the blessing of God on them. The Order of Blessing of the Sick differs from the visit to the sick in that the former provides a formula for the introduction and greeting and a series of intercessions, but the Lord's Prayer is omitted. Of course, it is certainly appropriate to pray the Our Father, perhaps after the intercessions. A priest, deacon, or lay person may lead the order of blessing. The form for the blessing of children follows the same order as the blessing for adults, although the intercessions are adapted for a child's level of understanding. The short form of blessing for children omits the intercessions and shortens both the

> The blessing of the sick by the ministers of the Church is a very ancient custom, having its origins in the practice of Christ himself and his apostles.
>
> —*Book of Blessings*, 376

introduction and the final blessing. All three blessings include a reading from Scripture. There is no requirement to offer a reflection on the reading although it is appropriate to do so. If a priest or deacon presides, he bestows a blessing on the sick person and those who are present. A lay presider signs the person and himself or herself with the Sign of the Cross and uses different words of blessing at the end of the celebration.

Orders for the Blessing of a Person Suffering from Addiction or from Substance Abuse

This order of blessing is "intended to strengthen the addicted person in the struggle to overcome addiction and also to assist his or her family and friends. . . . [It] may also be used for individuals who, although not addicted, abuse alcohol or drugs and wish the assistance of God's blessing in their struggle."[70] The pastoral care of someone who is struggling with addiction is much more demanding than the exercise of a blessing, as important as prayer is for them. The pastoral minister may use the occasion of the blessing to engage the person in conversation that might lead them, or at least encourage them, to seek additional help. The power of prayer is not to be discounted, but the powerful grip of addiction on one's health, including their spiritual well-being, is a great burden for the individual and those who are close to them. Any support that the pastoral minister is able to offer can benefit the person. A carefully worded homily or reflection on the Scripture texts can weave together the assurance of the Lord's care for the person with an exhortation for them to continue their own efforts to overcome their addiction.

The order of the blessing is a simple Liturgy of Word, with a longer and a shorter form. The words of the prayers that accompany the blessing are well chosen. Consider the impact that these words might have on a person in this situation: "Lord, / look with compassion on all those / who have lost their health and freedom. / Restore to them the assurance of your unfailing mercy, / strengthen them in the work of recovery."[71]

A priest, deacon, or lay person may preside at the blessing. The person may be sprinkled with holy water, if that seems appropriate. The minister extends his or her hands over the person in blessing. Although the rubrics do not call for the laying on of hands, often the sense of touch can convey an

---

70. BB, 407–408.
71. BB, 422B.

extra measure of care and support for the person. Those struggling with addiction sometimes feel that they struggle alone. The rite of blessing is its own expression of pastoral care and can be a visible and tangible sign of the compassion of the Lord.

Order for the Blessing of a Victim of Crime or Oppression

This blessing is intended "to assist the victim and help him or her come to a state of tranquility and peace."[72] Although the reference is singular, it may very well be that more than one person has been affected by a particular crime or an act of oppression (such as rape, gun violence, political disturbances, and so on). The order of blessing lends itself to a communal celebration and pastoral leaders might consider preparing the blessing to include any members of the parish or faith community who wish to participate. The liturgy team may take an active part in the preparation of the celebration. As with the situation that surrounds addiction, those who are victims of crime or oppression may very well need additional support from pastoral care ministers as well as from professional counselors. Those who plan a communal celebration need to be attentive to the actual circumstances when choosing Scripture texts, the intercessions, and any words of reflection. The choice of music, whether instrumental or sung, can be especially comforting. One or more extended moments of silence can be incorporated into the blessing. Healing takes many forms and takes time; there is no need to rush through such an important pastoral work as the healing of the human spirit.

Order for the Blessing of Parents before Childbirth

The *Book of Blessings* provides two orders of blessing that can be celebrated before childbirth. One is used when both parents are present; the other when only the mother is present. Since "a husband and wife participate in God's love through the sacrament of marriage and cooperate with the gift of life through the conception of a child, it is appropriate that they receive God's blessing together as they wait in faith and hope for the birth of their child."[73]

The blessing may be celebrated at any time during a pregnancy and a priest, deacon, or layperson may preside. The blessing takes the form of a Liturgy of the Word and the prayers and readings are especially appropriate

---

72. BB, 431.
73. BB, 215.

to the circumstances of expectant parents. The blessing may take place wherever it is convenient for the parents and any other family members or friends to gather—their home, a hospital setting, or the parish church. The blessing certainly lends itself to a communal celebration, and parish liturgy teams should schedule this blessing so that several expectant parents could be invited to participate (similar to Baptism preparation sessions). In such a situations, it is appropriate to include other liturgical ministers, for example a reader, music minister(s), and greeters. One of the parents could serve as reader and a couple who have already received this blessing, and given birth to their child, could serve as greeters.

> May the Son nourish your faith,
> build up your hope,
> and deepen in you the gift of his love.
> —*Book of Blessings*, 229

The minister who presides may give a brief reflection on the Scripture reading, emphasizing how every child is a sign of the grace of God in human life and encouraging the parents to be joyful and grateful for the new life that they have made possible.

Although a shorter rite is offered, the longer rite lends a more solemn and gracious tone to the occasion.

Orders for the Blessing of a Mother before and after Childbirth

This blessing is designed specifically for an individual mother.[74] The pastoral notes do not specify that this blessing is for a single mother; only that it is for the mother who is not accompanied by her husband or the father of the child. It could be that the father of the child is simply not able to be present. The celebration is also suitable for several mothers to gather for the blessing. A priest, deacon, or layperson can preside. The blessing can take place in any suitable place, including a hospital room or chapel, the parish church, or, when only one mother is present in her home. Other members of the family and friends may participate. An element in this rite not included in the blessing for parents is a prayer for protection by the Blessed Virgin. This invocation may be said or sung.[75] A shorter rite for this blessing is provided.

---

74. See BB, 236.
75. See BB, 250.

The Order for the Blessing of a Mother after Childbirth is offered to the mother when she is not able to participate in the celebration of the Sacrament of Baptism for her child.[76] This pastoral consideration addresses the situation where the mother's health after child birth prevents her from being present at the Baptism of her child. In practice, such a situation was more likely to occur in years past. Today, parents usually schedule a Baptism several weeks (or even months!) after the birth of their child when the mother and the child are well enough to participate in the celebration. The ritual text provides a shorter form of this blessing. The order of the blessing is in the form of a Liturgy of the Word; a priest, deacon, or layperson may offer the blessing.

Orders for the Blessing of Parents after a Miscarriage

The Church's pastoral ministers have a special interest in those who face the pain and loss brought about by the death of a loved one. This ministry is rooted in the compassion that Christ showed, in a very special way, to those who experienced brokenness in their lives. The death of any child, and the death of a child before birth, is a painful and poignant moment for parents.[77] This order of blessing is intended to offer consolation and prayerful support to parents who must cope with a miscarriage.[78]

The blessing is in the form of a Liturgy of the Word and the prayers and readings have been selected to bring as much comfort as possible to parents in their grief. A priest, deacon, or layperson may lead the order of blessing. Other persons may be present and invited to participate; although the parents will want to choose who should accompany them at this difficult time. Whoever leads the order of blessing should be fully aware of the circumstances surrounding the miscarriage so that they can be sensitive and supportive in their presence and in any remarks or reflections that they offer during the rite.[79] A short form of the blessing is also provided.

---

76. See BB, 258.

77. For an excellent reflection on the poignancy of this situation and the importance of ritual for healing see Herbert Anderson and Edward Foley, *"Unexpected Moments in the Life Cycle,"* in *Mighty Stories, Dangerous Rituals* (San Francisco: Jossey-Bass, 1998), 130.

78. See BB, 279–301.

79. The pastoral minister who attends to the parents in this situation should consult the Pastoral Notes in the Introduction to Funeral Rites for Children, *Order of Christian Funerals*, nn. 234–242. Since the parents may wish to discuss the funeral rites for their child at this time the pastoral minister should be able to assist with any questions and with the appropriate arrangements.

Distribution of Ashes to the Sick

The Order for the Blessing and Distribution of Ashes to the Sick is based on the Order of Blessing and Distribution of Ashes in *The Roman Missal*.[80] The rite is in the form of a Liturgy of the Word and can be celebrated in the place where the sick person is. The rite may be celebrated in its entirety by a priest or deacon apart from the liturgy, whether within Mass or outside Mass, that takes place in the church. If the pastoral visitor takes ashes that have already been blessed in a liturgy in the church, then the prayer of blessing is omitted. The rite may be abbreviated in other ways as well, but at least one Scripture reading should be included. A lay person may distribute blessed ashes to the sick; however, only a priest or deacon may invoke a blessing on the ashes

> Repent, and believe in the Gospel.
> —*The Roman Missal, Distribution of Ashes*

---

80. Pastoral ministers should be aware that the texts found in the *Book of Blessings* have not been updated since the promulgation of the third edition of *The Roman Missal*. Therefore, the responses and other necessary texts will need to be updated with those from the Missal.

RESOURCES

Church Documents and Ritual Books

Sacram Unctionem Infirmorum (The Holy Anointing of the Sick), 1972. This apostolic constitution officially promulgated the revised Rite of the Anointing of the Sick. It is found in the introductory pages of the ritual text.

Book of Blessings, 1987. The practice of blessing is an ancient and worthy tradition in the Church and the blessings in this collection express the belief of the Church that every good gift comes from God who sanctifies all people and all created things.

Catechism of the Catholic Church, second edition. United States Catholic Conference, 1997. The question and answer format of the *Catechism* provides an easy reference to explanations of the various aspects of the theology and the celebration of the Sacrament of the Anointing of the Sick. The answers are concise and the cross references are especially helpful. Refer to part 2, section 2, chapter 2, article 5: The Anointing of the Sick, 1499–1532.

Code of Canon Law, 1983. These canons deal with the canonical or legal aspects of the sacrament as well as the minister and the recipients of the sacrament: Book IV: The Sanctifying Office of the Church. Title VI: The Sacrament of Anointing the Sick. Canons 998–1007.

Directory for the Application of Principles and Norms on Ecumenism, 1993. This directory is an updated and expanded version of two previous post-Conciliar documents on ecumenism.

Evangelii Gaudium, 2013. This apostolic exhortation was issued by Pope Francis in the first year of his pontificate at the conclusion of the Year of Faith. The pope encourages the Christian faithful to "embark on a new chapter of evangelization" marked by the joy of the Gospel that "fills the hearts and lives of all who encounter Jesus."[1]

Guidelines for Celebrating the Sacraments with Persons with Disabilities, 1995, 2018. This document from the United States bishops addresses the issues that concern the pastoral care of persons with disabilities, especially their participation in and accessibility to the sacraments.

---

1. EG, 1.

Pastoral Care of the Sick: Rites of Anointing and Viaticum, 1972. The ritual book is available from the United States Conference of Catholic Bishops, Washington, DC. (It is also distributed by Liturgical Press, Liturgy Training Publications, and Catholic Book Publishing Corporation.)

Salvifici Doloris, 1984. In this apostolic letter, Pope John Paul II addresses the reality of human suffering in the experience of God's people. His particular focus is the salvific meaning of suffering found in the Scriptures, and especially the redemptive suffering of Jesus Christ, that liberates humankind from sin and death.

Varietates Legitimae (Inculturation and the Roman Liturgy), 1994. This is the fourth instruction on the application of the *Constitution on the Sacred Liturgy* and is directed primarily to conferences of bishops on the oversight and regulation of cultural adaptations in the liturgy.

Theological and Historical Resources

Anderson, Herbert, and Edward Foley. *Mighty Stories, Dangerous Rituals, Weaving Together the Human and the Divine.* San Francisco: Jossey-Bass Publishers, 1998. Drawing on their respective backgrounds of pastoral care and liturgy, Anderson and Foley explore the human elements of ritual and story and how they allow believers to cope with the passages of life. Their ability to weave memory, story, and ritual into a way to understand and celebrate the transitions of the human condition is superb.

Cooke, Bernard, and Gary Macy. *Christian Symbol and Ritual.* Oxford: Oxford University Press, 2005. Cooke and Macy present an excellent introduction to symbol and ritual, the foundational elements of sacramental theology and practice. Any understanding of sacrament needs to explore these two aspects of Christian liturgy. This book will not disappoint the serious student of the liturgy.

Glen, Genevieve, OSB, ed. *Recovering the Riches of Anointing: A Study of the Sacrament of the Sick.* Collegeville, MN: Liturgical Press, 2003. A collection of papers presented by various speakers of the National Association of Catholic Chaplains. The articles cover a range of topics that explore the theological and pastoral concerns of ministry to the sick.

Gusmer, C. *And You Visited Me: Sacramental Ministry to the Sick and Dying.* Collegeville, MN: Liturgical Press, 1984. Gusmer traces the history of the Sacrament of the Anointing of the Sick from its New Testament beginnings to the present reformed rites. His historical survey is concise and well researched and is an excellent source for anyone wanting to explore a thorough overview of this sacrament.

Irwin, Kevin W. *The Sacraments, Historical Foundations and Liturgical Theology.* Mahweh, NJ: Paulist Press, 2016. Irwin's scholarship in sacramental theology is well known and this treatment of the sacraments is a worthy testament to his expertise. He provides a solid survey on the history of the sacraments and then integrates the historical data with the developments in liturgical theology and pastoral practice in the life of the Church.

Kasza, John C. *Understanding Sacramental Healing: Anointing and Viaticum.* Chicago: Liturgy Training Publications, 2000. Kasza explores the rich history of the Sacrament of the Anointing of the Sick and addresses the changes that have occurred since the revised rite has been in use. He presents an overview of the post-Conciliar liturgical development with an emphasis on the pastoral implementation of the rite in the life of the parish.

Larson-Miller, Lizette. *The Sacrament of Anointing the Sick.* Collegeville, MN: Liturgical Press, 2005. Larson-Miller offers an extensive exploration of the biblical foundation for care of the sick and provides a thorough commentary on the elements of the rite of anointing. This is an excellent resource from the *Lex Orandi* series.

Martos, Joseph. *Doors to the Sacred: A Theological Introduction to the Sacraments in the Catholic Church.* Rev. ed. Liguori, Missouri: Liguori Publications, 2001. Chapter 10 in this resource provides an excellent treatment of the historical development of the Sacrament of the Anointing of the Sick, including an insightful exploration of the related issues that continue to face the Church today. The author provides an extensive bibliography at the end of the chapter.

Morrill, Bruce T. *Divine Worship and Human Healing, Liturgical Theology at the Margins of Life and Death.* Collegeville, MN: Liturgical Press, 2009. This work is without question one of finest treatments of the experience of human suffering and illness available. Morrill develops a systematic study of the rites of healing for the sick and dying as outlined in the ritual text. He sheds new light on the treasures of the Church's tradition of celebrating the divine mystery of healing.

Noll, Ray R. *Sacraments: A New Understanding for a New Creation.* Mystic, CT: Twenty-Third Publications, 1999. Noll's work explores the symbolic actions of each of the sacraments and presents some "what if" suggestions for pastoral practice. A CD-ROM with articles and passages from other theologians is included.

Smolarski, Dennis, csj. *Sacred Mysteries: Sacramental Principles and Liturgical Practice.* Mahweh, NJ: Paulist Press, 1995. Smolarski's primary interest is the ritual practice of the sacraments. He contends that in order to celebrate the sacraments well one needs an understanding of their history and a critical appreciation of the elements of the rites. He maintains that this can lead to a "healthy appreciation and reverence" for the celebration of sacramental rites. He treats the Sacrament of the Anointing of the Sick in chapter 8.

Ziegler, J. *Let Them Anoint the Sick*. Collegeville, MN: Liturgical Press, 1987. Ziegler deals with the three most common questions associated with this sacrament: Who may be anointed? Who can anoint? Why be anointed? He traces the history and thinking associated with the Anointing of the Sick and offers pastoral care ministers some new insights into the importance of this sacrament in the life of the Church.

Pastoral Resources

Ahlstrom, Michael P. "Comfort My People: Theological and Pastoral Reflections on the Care of the Sick and Dying." Chicago: *Chicago Studies* 43:1, Spring 2004. One of the questions associated with human suffering is "what does it mean?"; which is followed by the bigger question: "Why?" In this article, Ahlstrom comments on the theologies of suffering as well as on other pertinent pastoral issues that confront the pastoral care minister.

The Catholic Handbook for Visiting the Sick and Homebound is an annual publication designed for the lay pastoral minister published by Liturgy Training Publications. It includes all the rites, blessings, and prayers for pastoral care of the sick and dying. It also includes the Gospel of the Sundays throughout the year. One interesting feature is a list of ailments with the corresponding saint whose intercession is sought in time of illness.

Craghan, John F. *I Was Ill and You Cared for Me: Biblical Reflections on Serving the Physically and Mentally Impaired*. Collegeville, MN: Liturgical Press, 2014. The author combines reflections on his pastoral experiences with commentary on texts of Scripture. This is a good resource for meditation for pastoral ministers and others who accompany the sick.

———. "Human Suffering as a Theological and Pastoral Dilemma." *Chicago Studies* 43:1, Spring 2004. This issue of *Chicago Studies* includes five excellent articles on human suffering and pastoral care. Each article is a rich source of reflection for the pastoral care visitor, the homilist, and the student of Scripture.

Glen, Genevieve, OSB; Marilyn Kofler, SP; and Kevin O'Connor. *Handbook for Ministers of Care*. 2nd ed. Chicago: Liturgy Training Publications, 2007. This is a manual for those already involved in the ministry of care, and for those preparing to undertake this vital work. In these pages you will learn a theology of sickness and suffering, how the communion ritual works, practical advice on making pastoral visits, how to take care of yourself while caring for others, and where to find further information about illnesses affecting those you visit.

Horrigan, J. Philip. *Guide for Celebrating Reconciliation*. Chicago: Liturgy Training Publications, 2018. As part of the *Preparing Parish Worship* series, this resource provides pastoral insights for celebrating individual confession, communal Reconciliation services, and nonsacramental penance services with attention given to liturgical ministries, liturgical environment, and evangelization.

Kenny, Nuala, sc, md. *Rediscovering the Art of Dying: How Jesus' Experience and our Stories Reveal a New Vision of Compassionate Care*. Toronto: Novalis, 2017. Kenny's background in spirituality, medicine, and Christian ethics makes this work both timely and profound. This is a must have book for anyone who accompanies those who are suffering from illness and those who may be facing death.

Stice, Randy. *Understanding the Sacraments of Healing: A Rite-Based Approach*. Chicago: Liturgy Training Publications, 2015. Stice provides an introduction to sacramental theology and an exploration of the history and pastoral implications of that theology as it shapes the Sacrament of Reconciliation and the Anointing of the Sick. His treatment on living the sacrament offers an original insight on the Christian meaning of suffering.

GLOSSARY

Anoint: To apply oil as part of a liturgical rite.

Anointing of the Sick: The sacrament of healing for seriously ill individuals. Those whose health is seriously impaired by physical or mental sickness or age and request this sacrament are anointed with the oil of the sick so that they may be spiritually strengthened in their afflictions by Christ, who throughout his ministry healed those with various afflictions. It finds its biblical basis in James 5:14, which describes priests of the Church praying over the sick and anointing them. Before the Second Vatican Council, this sacrament was known as Extreme Unction.

Apostolic Pardon: A blessing, to which a plenary indulgence is attached, given before death for the remission of the temporal punishment due to sin. It is given in danger-of-death situations, usually with the reception of the Sacraments of Reconciliation and Anointing, including Viaticum.

Blessing: Any prayer that praises and thanks God. In particular, *blessing* describes those prayers in which God is praised because of some person or object, and thus the individual or object is seen to have become specially dedicated or sanctified because of the prayer of faith. Many blessing prayers ask God's favor toward a person in time of need or on a special occasion. Liturgical celebrations usually conclude with a blessing pronounced over the assembly.

Book of Blessings: The ritual book that contains blessings for numerous occasions, including visits to the sick. Many of the blessings may be given during the celebration of Mass, and so most of the rites include forms both for within Mass and outside Mass. In a number of cases, the rubrics specify that a lay minister may lead a particular ritual outside Mass.

Commendation of the Dying: The prayers for a dying person, found in *Pastoral Care of the Sick: Rites of Anointing and Viaticum.* The prayers are meant to assist the dying to face death with faith and trust by being united to Jesus' own death, and to bring consolation to those who are present. They include Scripture passages, the Litany of the Saints, and the Prayer of Commendation. The rites may be led by a priest, deacon, or layperson.

Exorcism: A rite or prayer used to cast out the presence of the devil. The *Rite of Exorcism* may only be used with the express permission of the bishop and only by mandated priest-exorcists.

Extraordinary Minister of Holy Communion: The liturgical minister who is authorized by the bishop to assist priests and deacons (who are the ordinary ministers of Communion) in the distribution of Holy Communion. An extraordinary minister functions when a sufficient number of ordinary ministers is not present. These ministers may also be dismissed from Mass to give Communion to the sick and homebound.

Extreme Unction: The name used before the revision of the sacraments after the Second Vatican Council for the sacrament now called the Anointing of the Sick. This former name emphasized the previous common practice of delaying the reception of the sacrament until the moment of death, so that it was truly the last (*extreme*) anointing (*unction*).

Holy Communion and Worship of the Eucharist outside Mass: The ritual book that gives the norms and rubrics for the distribution of Holy Communion outside Mass, and the rites for the worship of the Eucharist outside Mass. The rubrics for Exposition and Benediction of the Blessed Sacrament can be found here as well as information concerning Eucharistic processions and Eucharistic Congresses.

Last Rites: Although more commonly used before the Second Vatican Council, this term refers to the reception of the Sacraments of Penance, Anointing of the Sick, and Viaticum prior to one's death.

Laying On of Hands: A gesture of blessing or invocation mentioned in the New Testament in conjunction with prayer (see Acts 13:3; 2 Timothy 1:6). The gesture is performed by extending both hands forward with the palms turned downward. Depending on the circumstances, the hands may be placed on the person's head or stretched out over a group of people or over an object. The gesture is used in many of the sacraments to indicate the conferral of special grace or the invocation of the Holy Spirit, as at Ordination and Confirmation, during absolution in the Sacrament of Penance, and at the invocation of the Spirit during a Eucharistic Prayer. The same gesture is also used during a solemn blessing or prayer over the people at the conclusion of Mass.

Oil of the Sick: One of the three holy oils. It is used to anoint the sick, usually on the forehead and on the palms of the hands, in the celebration of the Anointing of the Sick. It is stored in a decanter or oil stock labeled OI, for *oleum infirmorum,* "oil of the sick."

Pastoral Care of the Sick: Rites of Anointing and Viaticum: Ritual book that is part of the *Roman Ritual* and gives the rites for ministering to the sick and dying. Included are rites for visiting the sick, for bringing Holy Communion to the sick, for the Sacrament of the Anointing of the Sick, and for ministering to the dying and at the time of death. Many of the rites in this book may be led by deacons or by laypersons in addition to priests.

Penance: (1) The sacrament by which the baptized, through the mercy of God, receive pardon for their sins and reconciliation with the Church. This sacrament is most commonly celebrated by the private confession of sin and expression of sorrow by a penitent to a confessor, who then offers absolution. It is also commonly called confession or the Sacrament of Reconciliation. (2) An act of satisfaction, or atonement, imposed on a penitent by the confessor as part of the Sacrament of Penance.

Praenotanda: The introductory texts in a ritual book, such as the *General Instruction of the Roman Missal.* Such texts usually have the title "Introduction" or "General Introduction" and provide important theological foundations and explanations for the ritual, along with norms, rubrics, and other instructions.

Pyx: A vessel used to carry consecrated bread for Holy Communion to the sick.

Reconciliation: An action of healing relationships wounded in some way; used in a liturgical sense to refer to the reestablishment of a right relationship between God and the human race through the life, death, and Resurrection of Jesus Christ. The term is commonly used as a title for the Sacrament of Penance, or confession.

Rite of Penance: The ritual book, part of the *Roman Ritual,* that provides the rites for the celebration of the Sacrament of Penance. Included are the Rite of Reconciliation of Individual Penitents, the Rite of Reconciliation of Several Penitents with Individual Confession and Absolution, the Rite for Reconciliation of Several Penitents with General Confession and Absolution, and sample penitential services.

Ritual Masses: A category of Mass formularies found in *The Roman Missal* to be used when sacraments and other rituals are celebrated within Mass. Examples include Masses for the Conferral of the Sacraments of Initiation, for the Conferral of the Anointing of the Sick, and for Religious Profession.

Sacramentals: Sacred signs, including words, actions, and objects that signify spiritual effects achieved through the intercession of the Church. Unlike the sacraments, which have been instituted by Christ, sacramentals are instituted by the Church. Sacramentals include blessings, medals, statues and other sacred images, palms, holy water, and many devotions, including the Rosary. They prepare us to receive the fruit of the sacraments and sanctify different circumstances of life.[2]

Sacraments of Healing: The Sacraments of Penance and Anointing of the Sick, as described in the *Catechism of the Catholic Church*. Through the ministry of the Church, they continue the Lord's work of healing and salvation.

Sacrarium: A special sink, usually with an attached cover, whose drain goes directly into the ground rather than into a sewer, found in the sacristy of a church. Its purpose is primarily the disposal of water used for cleansing the sacred vessels and other items that come in contact with the Eucharistic elements.

Serious Illness: The Sacrament of the Anointing of the Sick may be given to those who are facing a serious illness, such as cancer, surgery, or even serious mental illnesses.

Viaticum: Latin for "provisions for a journey." Viaticum is Holy Communion received before death as food and nourishment for the journey to heaven; it may be celebrated within or outside Mass. The rite for the giving of Communion as Viaticum also gives the sick person the opportunity to renew his or her baptismal profession of faith. Viaticum is the last sacrament, administered after the Anointing of the Sick.

---

2. See *Catechism of the Catholic Church*, 1677.

ACKNOWLEDGMENTS

Scripture readings are from the *New American Bible*, revised edition © 2010, 1991, 1986, 1970 Confraternity of Christian Doctrine, Washington, DC. Used with permission. All rights reserved. No part of the *New American Bible* may be reproduced without permission in writing from the copyright owner.

Excerpts from *Documents on the Liturgy, 1963-1979: Conciliar, Papal, and Curial Texts* © 1982, International Commission on English in the Liturgy Corporation (ICEL); excerpts from the English translation of *Pastoral Care of the Sick: Rites of Anointing and Viaticum* © 1982, ICEL; excerpts from the English translation of *Order of Christian Funerals* © 1985, 1989, ICEL; excerpts from the English translation of *Book of Blessings* © 1987, ICEL; excerpts from the English translation of *The Roman Missal* © 2010, ICEL; excerpts from the English translation of *Exorcisms and Related Supplications* © 2014, ICEL. All rights reserved. Texts contained in this work derived whole or in part from liturgical texts copyrighted by the International Commission on English in the Liturgy (ICEL) have been published here with the confirmation of the Committee on Divine Worship, United States Conference of Catholic Bishops. No other texts in this work have been formally reviewed or approved by the United States Conference of Catholic Bishops.

The Glossary definitions were written by Dennis C. Smolarski, sj, and Joseph DeGrocco © Liturgy Training Publications.